SCHOLASTIC

50 IDEAS FOR ABLE MATHEMATICIANS

- Age appropriate lessons to stretch confident learners
- Ideas to accelerate progress through objectives
- Bank of challenging brainteasers

AGES 9-11

Bob Ansell

Credits

Author
Bob Ansell

Editor
Chrisitine Vaughan
Kim Vernon
Sara Wiegand

Assistant Editor
John Billam

Illustrations
Phil Garner

Series Designer
Catherine Perera

Designer
Marjolein Liesker

Text © 2007 Bob Ansell
© 2007 Scholastic Ltd

Designed using Adobe InDesign

Published by Scholastic Ltd
Villiers House
Clarendon Avenue
Leamington Spa
Warwickshire CV32 5PR

www.scholastic.co.uk

Printed by Bell and Bain Ltd, Glasgow.

1 2 3 4 5 6 7 8 9   7 8 9 0 1 2 3 4 5 6

British Library Cataloguing-in-Publication Data
A catalogue record for this book is available from the British Library.

ISBN 978-0439-94529-5

The right of Bob Ansell to be identified as the author of this work has been asserted by him in accordance with the Copyright, Designs and Patents Act 1988.

Extracts from Primary National Strategy's *Primary Framework for Mathematics* (2006) www.standards.dfes.gov.uk/primaryframework © Crown copyright. Reproduced under the terms of the Click Use Licence.

Contents

About the series

50 Maths Lessons for More Able Learners is a series of three books designed for teachers working with higher ability children within the daily mathematics lesson. Each title will address the principles of inclusion for more confident learners identified in *Excellence and Enjoyment: Learning and Teaching in the Primary Years* (DfES, 2004). Each book covers a two-year span of the primary age range: KS1 5-7 and KS2 7-9 and 9-11.

Each title consists of 20 short 'brainteaser' activities and 50 lesson plans, each with an accompanying photocopiable activity page. The activities cover many of the objectives in the Primary National Strategy's revised *Primary Framework for Mathematics* (2006). The lesson plans and accompanying photocopiable activities are designed to:
- set suitable learning challenges for more able learners
- accelerate progress through learning objectives
- provide tasks that are more open-ended or extended in time and complexity
- fit into the individual teacher's existing planning for mathematics.

How to use this book

This book begins with a detailed Objectives grid, giving an overview of the objectives addressed by each lesson. Teachers can also use this grid to track forward to identify appropriate objectives from later years where necessary.

Brainteaser activities

A bank of 20 brainteaser activities follows (with linked photocopiable sheets on pages 18-27). The purpose of these activities is to provide short, focused opportunities to stretch more able pupils. Where relevant, links to brainteaser activities are included on the lesson plans. However, they can also be used flexibly as required – for example, you may want to map similar brainteasers with the theme of a lesson, or extend learning as a homework or assessment task.

Lesson plans

To make the book easy to use, all 50 lesson plans follow the same format:

Learning objectives

Each lesson is written to address one or more of the PNS strands from Years 5 and 6. Where appropriate, objective links to Year 7 are also included.

Expected prior knowledge

This incorporates a brief summary of what children should be expected to know or do before starting each lesson.

Key vocabulary

Key mathematical vocabulary linked to the PNS Framework (2006) is presented for each lesson.

Activity introduction

Each lesson opens with a short introduction, designed to introduce the context of the lesson to the group (NB: these activities would not be suitable for the whole class). The introduction can also be used to review requirements in terms of mathematical understanding and to facilitate or scaffold thinking. Although the teacher will be at the centre of this section of the lesson, the main purpose is to pose questions and lines of enquiry for the children to develop during the main activity.

Introduction

Activity development

Incorporating instructions for setting and developing the main activity, this section offers opportunities for children to explain their thinking, so a range of teacher questions has been included. It is intended that the teacher will be at the perimeter of the group, allowing the children to maintain ownership of the learning, but will be available for low-level interventions. These include making observations, highlighting teaching/learning points, providing hints or tips for solving problems, suggesting methods of recording and so on.

Review

This section is focused upon allowing children to explain their thinking or present their work, so that effective formative and summative assessment can be made. It also reviews all possible outcomes to an activity and summarises key learning points.

Next steps

At the end of each lesson plan, ideas are included for how to develop an activity further. These ideas include at least one modification to an activity designed to challenge children and extend learning. This section also includes links to thinking skills and ICT.

Characteristics of able children

An able child may demonstrate potential in a variety of ways:
- cognitive skills (for example, learning new ideas with extraordinary speed)
- speech and language, such as ability to follow a complex set of instructions
- learning styles (for example, logical approaches to problems)
- social, such as high expectations of self/others.

In mathematics, this might manifest itself through content (such as making links within and across different topics) and/or through process (for example, an aptitude for solving logical problems).

Interventions

In extending able learners through challenge, pace and expectation, it is also important to consider the value of breadth of content. Most of the activities featured in this book include themes that all children in the class are likely to be exploring, albeit at a lower level of complexity. This feature enables the able child or group to integrate with the on-going topics of the class, and this serves an important social function.

An able child represents a challenge in terms of establishing the nature and extent of support. Broadly speaking, an able child needs every bit as much focus on learning as any other child. Through intervention and discussion, an able child can begin to appreciate what outcomes are expected or valued.

Curriculum initiatives

One of the key objectives within *Excellence and Enjoyment* (DfES, 2004) was to support schools in taking ownership of the curriculum. This includes developing teaching programmes which support all groups, and in shaping the curriculum in ways which will maximise opportunity and achievement. Within this, the Primary National Strategy is seen as a vehicle to develop assessment for learning, providing knowledge about individual children to inform the way they are taught and learn. This book supports these aspirations by providing a measured approach to extending the more able child and, as appropriate, to engage directly with that individual in this process.

Title of lesson	Year 5 objectives	Year 6 objectives	Year 6/7 objectives
1. Tricky towers		Use/apply strand: Explain reasoning and conclusions, using symbols where appropriate.	
2. Intersecting loops (1)	Use/apply strand: Solve one- and two-step problems involving whole numbers. Use/apply strand: Explain reasoning using diagrams; refine ways of recording using images and symbols.		
3. Intersecting loops (2)	Use/apply strand: Solve one- and two-step problems involving whole numbers.		Use/apply strand: (For 'Next steps' only) Develop and evaluate lines of enquiry; identify, collect, organise and analyse relevant information; decide how best to represent conclusions and what further questions to ask.
4. Fraction squeeze	Counting strand: Express a smaller whole number as a fraction of a larger one; relate fractions to their decimal representations.		Counting strand: Order a set of fractions by converting them to decimals.
5. Ordering fractions	Counting strand: Express a smaller whole number as a fraction of a larger one; relate fractions to their decimal representations.		Counting strand: Order a set of fractions by converting them to decimals.
6. Pipes	Use/apply strand: Solve one- and two-step problems involving whole numbers and decimals and all four operations, choosing and using appropriate calculation strategies. Counting strand: Count from any given number in whole-number and decimal steps. Knowledge strand: Identify pairs of factors of two-digit whole numbers and find common multiples.		
7. Sequences (1)	Counting strand: Count from any given number in whole-number steps, extending beyond zero when counting backwards; relate the numbers to their position on a number line.		
8. Sequences (2)		Use/apply strand: Represent and interpret sequences, patterns and relationships involving numbers; suggest and test hypotheses.	
9. Make a big difference	Use/apply strand: Solve one- and two-step problems involving whole numbers.	Knowledge strand: Use knowledge of place value and multiplication facts to derive related facts.	
10. Missing numbers	Knowledge strand: Recall quickly multiplication facts up to 10 × 10. Use/apply strand: Represent a problem by identifying and recording the calculations needed to solve it; find possible solutions and confirm them in the context of the problem.		
11. Factor trees	Knowledge strand: Identify pairs of factors of two-digit whole numbers and find common multiples, eg for 6 and 9.	Knowledge strand: Recognise that prime numbers have only two factors and identify prime numbers less than 100; find the prime factors of two-digit numbers.	
12. Cuboid numbers	Use/apply strand: Explore patterns, properties and relationships and propose a general statement involving numbers. Knowledge strand: Identify pairs of factors of two-digit whole numbers and find common multiples.	Knowledge strand: Recognise that prime numbers have only two factors and identify prime numbers less than 100; find the prime factors of two-digit whole numbers.	
13. Divisibility tests	Knowledge strand: Recall quickly multiplication facts up to 10 × 10 and use them to multiply pairs of multiples of 10 and 100; derive quickly corresponding division facts. Knowledge strand: Identify pairs of factors of two-digit whole numbers and find common multiples.		
14. Sieving for primes	Knowledge strand: Identify pairs of factors of two-digit whole numbers and find common multiples, eg for 6 and 9.	Knowledge strand: Recognise that prime numbers have only two factors and identify prime numbers less than 100.	

Title of lesson	Year 5 objectives	Year 6 objectives	Year 6/7 objectives
15. The square root of 12		**Use/apply strand:** Solve multi-step problems involving decimals; choose and use appropriate (and efficient) strategies at each stage, including calculator use. **Knowledge strand:** Use approximations, inverse operations and tests of divisibility to check results. **Calculate strand:** Use a calculator to solve problems involving multi-step calculations.	**Knowledge strand:** Make and justify estimates and approximations to calculations.
16. Decimal divison	**Use/apply strand:** Solve one- and two-step problems involving whole numbers and decimals and all four operations, choosing and using appropriate methods, including calculator use.	**Calculate strand:** Calculate mentally with whole numbers and decimals, eg U.t + U.t, TU × U, TU ÷ U, U.t × U, HU.t ÷ U.	**Calculate strand:** Consolidate and extend mental methods of calculation to include decimals.
17. Grid tricks	**Calculate strand:** Refine and use efficient written methods to multiply HTU × U, TU × TU and U.t ÷ U.		
18. Sweet stuff		**Use/apply strand:** Explain reasoning and conclusions, using symbols as appropriate.	
19. Broken calculator			**Use/apply strand:** Solve problems by breaking down complex calculations into simpler steps; choose and use operations and calculation strategies appropriate to the numbers and context; try alternative approaches to overcome difficulties; present, interpret and compare solutions. **Calculate strand:** Understand how the commutative and distributive laws, and the relationships between operations can be used to calculate more efficiently; use the order of operations, including brackets.
20. Can you trust your calculator?		**Use/apply strand:** Solve multi-step problems; choose and use appropriate calculation strategies at each stage, including calculator use. **Calculate strand:** Use a calculator to solve problems involving multi-step calculations.	**Calculate strand:** Understand how the distributive law can be used to calculate more efficiently; use the order of operations, including brackets.
21 Chocolate fudge cake	**Use/apply:** Solve one- and two-step problems involving whole numbers and decimals and all four operations, choosing and using appropriate calculation strategies, including calculator use. **Calculate strand:** Find fractions using division and percentages of numbers and quantities. **Calculate strand:** Use a calculator to solve problems, including those involving decimals or fractions; interpret the display correctly in the context of measurement.		
22. How big is a million?		**Use/apply strand:** Solve multi-step problems, and problems involving fractions, decimals and percentages; choose and use appropriate calculation strategies at each stage, including calculator use. **Calculate strand:** Use a calculator to solve problems involving multi-step calculations.	
23. Arithmagons	**Use/apply strand:** Explore patterns, properties and relationships and propose a general statement involving numbers or shapes; identify examples for which the statement is true or false.	**Use/apply strand:** Represent and interpret sequences, patterns and relationships involving numbers; suggest and test hypotheses.	
24. Logical loops		**Use/apply strand:** Solve multi-step problems, and problems involving fractions, decimals and percentages; choose and use appropriate calculation strategies at each stage, including calculator use. **Use/apply strand:** Explain reasoning and conclusions, using words, symbols or diagrams as appropriate. **Calculate strand:** Find fractions and percentages of whole-number quantities.	
25. You've been framed	**Use/apply strand:** Represent a problem by identifying and recording the calculations needed to solve it; find possible solutions and confirm them in the context of the problem.	**Use/apply strand:** Solve multi-step problems, and problems involving fractions, decimals and percentages, choose and use appropriate and efficient methods at each stage, including calculator use.	

Title of lesson	Year 5 objectives	Year 6 objectives	Year 6/7 objectives
26. Trains		**Use/apply strand**: Solve multi-step problems; choose and use appropriate calculation strategies at each stage.	
27. Substitution codes	**Use/apply strand**: Represent a problem by identifying and recording the calculations needed to solve it; find possible solutions and confirm them in the context of the problem.	**Use/apply strand**: Tabulate systematically the information in a problem or puzzle; identify and record the calculations needed to solve it, using symbols where appropriate; interpret solutions in the original context and check their accuracy.	
28. Make nine	**Use/apply strand**: Represent a problem by identifying and recording the information or calculations needed to solve it; find possible solutions and confirm them in the context of the problem. **Use/apply strand**: Explore patterns, properties and relationships and propose a general statement involving numbers.		
29. Domino puzzles	**Use/apply strand**: Solve one- and two-step problems involving whole numbers and decimals and all four operations, choosing and using appropriate calculation strategies. **Use/apply strand**: Represent a problem by identifying and recording the calculations needed to solve it; find possible solutions and confirm them in the context of the problem.	**Use/apply strand**: Tabulate systematically the information in a problem or puzzle; identify and record the steps or calculations needed to solve it, using symbols where appropriate; interpret solutions in the original context and check their accuracy.	
30. Hexagon puzzles	**Shape strand**: Identify, visualise and describe properties of rectangles, triangles and regular polygons; use knowledge of properties to draw 2D shapes.		
31. Lost bears	**Shape strand**: Read and plot coordinates in the first quadrant; recognise parallel and perpendicular lines in grids and shapes.	**Shape strand**: Use coordinates in the first quadrant to draw and locate shapes.	
32. Missing corners			**Shape strand**: Find coordinates of points determined by geometric information.
33. Quadrilateral properties		**Shape strand**: Describe, identify and visualise parallel and perpendicular edges or faces; use these properties to classify 2D shapes.	
34. Symmetrical squares		**Shape strand**: Visualise and draw on grids of different types where a shape will be after reflection or after rotation through 90° or 180° about its centre or one of its vertices.	
35. Treasure hunt		**Shape strand**: Use coordinates in the first quadrant to draw and locate shapes.	**Shape strand**: Find coordinates of points determined by geometric information.
36. Diagonals		**Use/apply strand**: Tabulate systematically the information in a problem or puzzle; identify and record the steps or calculations needed to solve it, using symbols where appropriate; interpret solutions in the original context and check their accuracy. **Shape strand**: Make and draw shapes with increasing accuracy and apply knowledge of their properties.	
37. Pick's theorem		**Use/apply strand**: (Represent a problem) ... identify and record the steps and calculations needed to solve it, using symbols where appropriate; interpret solutions in the original context and check their accuracy. **Shape strand**: Make and draw shapes with increasing accuracy and apply knowledge of their properties.	
38. Euler's formula	**Shape strand**: Identify, visualise and describe properties of regular polygons and 3D solids.	**Shape strand**: Describe, identify and visualise parallel and perpendicular edges or faces; use these properties to classify 3D solids. **Shape strand**: Make and draw shapes with increasing accuracy and apply knowledge of their properties.	
39. Platonic solids	**Shape strand**: Identify, visualise and describe properties of regular polygons and 3D solids.	**Shape strand**: Describe, identify and visualise parallel and perpendicular edges or faces and use these properties to classify 3D solids. **Shape strand**: Make and draw shapes with increasing accuracy and apply knowledge of their properties.	
40. Crossing the country	**Use/apply strand**: Explain reasoning, using diagrams, graphs and text. **Measure strand**: Read timetables and time using 24-hour clock notation.		

Title of lesson	Year 4 objectives	Year 5 objectives	Tracking forward Year 6 objectives
41. Paper sizes	**Use/apply strand:** Explore patterns, properties and relationships and propose a general statement involving numbers or shapes. **Measure strand:** Draw and measure lines to the nearest millimetre; measure and calculate the perimeter of regular and irregular polygons; use the formula for the area of a rectangle to calculate its area.	**Measure strand:** Use standard metric units of measure and convert between units using decimals to two places (eg change 2.75 litres to 2750ml, or vice versa).	
42. Paper weight		**Use/apply strand:** Solve multi-step problems, and problems involving fractions and decimals; choose and use appropriate (and efficient) calculation strategies at each stage, including calculator use. **Measure strand:** Select and use standard metric units of measure and convert between units using decimals to two places.	
43. Unusual measuring	**Measure strand:** Read, choose, use and record standard metric units to estimate and measure length, weight and capacity to a suitable degree of accuracy; convert larger to smaller units using decimals to one place (eg change 2.6kg to 2600g). **Measure strand:** Draw and measure lines to the nearest millimetre; use the formula for the area of a rectangle to calculate its area. **Knowledge strand:** Use knowledge of rounding, place value and number facts to estimate and to check calculations.		
44. Getting to school		**Data strand:** Solve problems involving selecting, processing, presenting and interpreting data; draw conclusions and identify further questions to ask. **Data strand:** Interpret pie charts.	**Data strand:** Interpret and compare graphs and diagrams that represent data, for example compare two proportions in two pie charts that represent different totals.
45. How strong is a bridge	**Data strand:** (Determine the data needed to) answer a set of related questions by selecting and organising relevant data; using ICT to present (and highlight) features, and identify further questions to ask.	**Use/apply strand:** Tabulate systematically the information in a problem or puzzle. **Data strand:** Construct and interpret line graphs.	
46. Toppling cubes	**Data strand:** Answer a set of related questions by collecting, selecting and organising relevant data; using ICT to present (and highlight) features and identify further questions to ask.	**Use/apply strand:** Tabulate systematically the information in a problem or puzzle.	
47. How fast is that?		**Use/apply strand:** Solve multi-step problems, and problems involving fractions, decimals and percentages; choose and use appropriate calculation strategies at each stage, including calculator use. **Measure strand:** Compare readings on different scales. **Data strand:** Describe and interpret results and solutions to problems using the mode, range, median and mean.	
48. Dicing with probability (1)	**Data strand:** Describe the occurrence of familiar events using the language of chance or likelihood.	**Data strand:** Describe and predict outcomes from data using the language of chance or likelihood.	**Data strand:** Understand and use the probability scale from 0 to 1; find and justify probabilities based on equally likely outcomes in simple contexts.
49. Dicing with probability (2)	**Data strand:** Describe the occurrence of familiar events using the language of chance or likelihood.	**Data strand:** Describe and predict outcomes from data using the language of chance or likelihood.	**Data strand:** Understand and use the probability scale from 0 to 1; find and justify probabilities based on equally likely outcomes in simple contexts.
50. Probable pairs		**Data strand:** Describe and predict outcomes from data using the language of chance or likelihood. **Data strand:** Solve problems by selecting, processing, presenting and interpreting data; draw conclusions and identify further questions to ask.	**Data strand:** Understand and use the probability scale from 0 to 1; find and justify probabilities based on equally likely outcomes in simple contexts.

SELF ASSESSMENT ▢ RECORDING SHEET

Name: _____   Date: _____

Activity title:			
I can _____ _____ _____ _____ _____ _____	👍	✊	👎
I was able to _____ _____ _____ _____ _____ _____	👍	✊	👎

I can

_____

_____

_____

	Use/apply strand	Counting strand	Knowledge strand	Calculate strand	Shape strand	Measure strand	Data strand
1. Factors			●				
2. Domino squares	●						
3. How many dominoes?	●						
4. Arithmagon investigation	●						
5. Target numbers			●	●			
6. 1001 calculations	●		●				
7. How old is Gran?	●			●			
8. Leaky tank	●	●					
9. Make 15	●						
10. One penny left over	●			●			
11. Last one loses	●						
12. No change from a pound	●						
13. Diagonal sums	●						
14. Right-angled puzzle	●						
15. Dice with a difference	●						●
16. Think of a number				●			
17. Paper folding	●				●		
18. The missing square	●				●		
19. Hidden shapes					●		
20. Find the fruit	●						

Brainteasers

1 Factors

Thinking skills: Reasoning about number and calculation.

What to do: Children may approach this activity in a variety of ways. Some may list multiples of some or all of the factors. Some may even have an intuitive sense of the type of number which is likely to have several factors.

Probing questions: What are some of the properties of the number you are looking for? Is there a way to produce the number by using the factors?

Outcomes: The only two-digit solution is 60. With three digits and the number seven included in the list the smallest solution will be a multiple of the primes, 2, 3, 5, and 7. Hence we need multiples of $2 \times 3 \times 5 \times 7 = 210$. This gives us the four three-digit solutions 210, 420, 630 and 840.

Next step: Give the children a different set of factors to work with. Increasing or decreasing the number of factors allows for differentiation.

2 Domino squares

Thinking skills: Reasoning about number patterns and calculations.

What to do: Children use a full set of 28 dominoes. They create seven square loops of four dominoes each. Where dominoes join the number of spots must be the same on each domino. If children cannot find a complete solution, award them a point for each loop they complete.

Probing questions: Are there any good dominoes to start the pattern off with? How can you make good use of the doubles?

Outcomes: There are several ways to produce seven square loops. Ask the children to record their solution so that other children may check it.

Next step: Lay out seven square loops so that the sum of the spots along each side of the square is the same.

Learning objective
(Y6) Use/apply strand:
Tabulate systematically the information in a problem or puzzle; identify and record the steps or calculations needed to solve it, using symbols where appropriate; interpret solutions in the original context and check their accuracy.

3 How many dominoes?

Thinking skills: Reasoning about number and calculation.

What to do: Children use a full set of 28 dominoes. They create an ordered triangle.

Probing questions: What is special about the arrangement of numbers on a domino? Is there a way to set them out so that it is easier to spot a pattern? How is the number of dominoes in the set related to the highest number of spots on a domino?

Outcomes: If necessary encourage the children to set the dominoes out in a triangle. This will illustrate that 28 is a triangle number. For those children who can understand the generalisation explain that the number of dominoes in a double-six set can be found by calculating 7×8 and halving the answer. A double-nine set has $10 \times 11 \div 2 = 55$, and a double-twelve set has $13 \times 14 \div 2 = 91$. The set with 66 dominoes is a double-ten set.

Next step: Invite the children to approach the problem with more extensive use of symbols.

Learning objective
(Y6) Use/apply strand:
Tabulate systematically the information in a problem or puzzle; identify and record the steps or calculations needed to solve it, using symbols where appropriate; interpret solutions in the original context and check their accuracy.

4 Arithmagon investigation

Thinking skills: Reasoning about number and calculation.

What to do: The children first need to understand what an arithmagon is. They make a series of them using one set of digit cards. They need to check for duplicates. Other children can check that each one is correct and is not one of those already found, but transformed by rotation or reflection.

Probing questions: How can you be systematic when tackling this problem? How can you check for duplicates? What would a reflected or rotated duplicate look like?

Outcomes: A record of each one found can be displayed for others to check. In this way a large group can contribute to the task of finding them all.

Next step: Is it possible to make a square arithmagon with just one set of cards? If so then make one. If not then explain why.

Learning objectives
(Y5) Knowledge strand: Use knowledge of place value and addition and subtraction of two-digit numbers to derive sums and differences.
(Y5) Calculate strand: Extend mental methods for whole-number calculations.

5 Target numbers

Thinking skill: Making effective use of numbers and operations to achieve a target.

What to do: Give the children the digit cards 1 to 5 and the operation symbols +, - and ×. The children need to use all of the five digits and any number of symbols to create calculations answers from 1 to 20.

Probing questions: Is there a good way to pair some numbers? (For example you can add one by adding four and subtracting three.) Why do we need brackets? (The children could be invited to use both a four-function calculator and a scientific calculator to check their answers and comment on the differences.)

Outcomes: All results are possible between 1 and 20. Indeed most of them can be made in several ways.

Next step: Invite the children to try to find answers above 20. They can be reminded of the power of the distributive law for generating larger numbers. For example $5 \times (3 + 4) = 35$.

6 1001 calculations

Thinking skill: Reasoning about a number problem.

What to do: The children are to use a mathematical 'trick' to try to impress a partner with their lightning calculation skills. The main activity then becomes trying to discover how it works. The reasons are given below in the Outcomes section.

Probing questions: What is special about the six-digit number? What do you get when you multiply together 7, 11 and 13? How is this useful?

Outcomes: The calculation will always yield 13 as an answer since a six-digit number made from three digits repeated will always be a multiple of 1001. In the example used on the pupil sheet:
347 347 = 347 × 1001 = 347 × 7 × 11 × 13.

Next step: To give some variation the children can ask for the six-digit number to be divided first by 7 then by 13 and then by the original number. The result will be 11. A similar procedure can be used but with division by 11 and 13 to give an answer of 7.

7 How old is Gran?

Thinking skills: Reasoning about number and calculation.

What to do: Encourage the children to read the problem through carefully and to discuss it before deciding what calculations are needed to solve it.

Probing questions: How does the information in each statement help you? How can you find out what calculations you need to do?

Outcomes: The grandmother is 54, mother 27 and the girl is 9. A systematic way to approach this is to work backwards a little. Start with the girl. Let her age be n. The mother is $3n$ and grandmother, being twice as old as mother, is $6n$. If we add all of these up, we get $10n$. We know that $10n = 90$; $90 \div 10 = 9$ so $n = 9$. Dad is 30. His age is simply the total age, 90, divided by 3.

Next step: Invite the children to make up stories or examples of their own. They must be careful to make sure that the problem is possible and that ages make sense.

8 Leaky tank

Thinking skill: Use proportional reasoning within the context of number.

What to do: Make sure the children understand the context of the problem and have some ideas about how to tackle it. Allow plenty of discussion time and time to experiment. The final question may be too demanding for many children and could be kept for a 'Next step' or a whole-group discussion.

Probing questions: How can we combine the information about the two taps? What effect does the hole have on the calculations? Is there a way of converting the information so that it is easier to use?

Outcomes: By converting the flow from the taps into 'tanks per hour', we can see that tap A fills at one tank per hour, tap B fills at two tanks per hour, so they fill three tanks per hour between them. At this rate the tank will fill in one third of an hour, or 20 minutes. The effect of the leak is equivalent to emptying it at the rate of 0.5 tanks per hour. This makes the overall filling rate 2.5 tanks per hour. If we divide one hour by 2.5 we get 24 minutes.

Next step: Use the final part of the problem as a next step. Alternatively, invite the children to calculate how long the tank would take to fill with tap A and the leak, and then tap B and the leak. You could introduce a more dramatic leak to complicate the situation. For example, if the leak is such as to empty the tank in 24 minutes, how long does it take to fill now?

9 Make 15

Thinking skill: Reasoning about a number problem in the context of a puzzle or game.

What to do: The activity is presented as a game between two players. However, it could be tackled by one person as a puzzle, in which the objective is to determine a winning strategy.

Probing questions: Are any numbers more use than others? Is there a relationship between odd and even numbers in sums to 15?

Outcomes: After playing and investigating the game the children may notice how the sum of 15 is made from a mixture of odd and even numbers. There are strong links between this activity and a magic square.

Next step: Make a magic square with the numbers 1 to 9. What is the magic total? Make a connection between the arrangement of numbers in your magic square and your strategy for winning this game.

Learning objectives
(Y6) Use/apply strand: Tabulate systematically the information in a problem or puzzle; identify and record the steps or calculations needed to solve it; interpret solutions in the original context and check their accuracy.

10 One penny left over

Thinking skills: Use reasoning within the context of a problem. Extract the mathematics required from the context of a problem.

What to do: Invite the children to extract the mathematics from the problem. The problem is really about finding a number which has a remainder of 1 when divided by 2, 3, 4, 5, and 6. Children may find translating the problem into an abstract mathematical one difficult and they may prefer to retain the context. It may be helpful to give children a large pile of cubes or counters to allow them to model the problem.

Probing questions: Can you translate the problem into one just involving numbers? Do you have to use all of the information to solve the problem?

Outcomes: The children are seeking a number which is one more than a multiple of, 2, 3, 4, 5, and 6. The numbers 2 and 3 can be ignored as they are dealt with by the multiples of 6. This makes the problem more manageable. One solution can be found readily as 4 × 5 × 6 + 1. But this is more than 100 (or £1). Further investigation shows that since both 4 and 6 have a factor of 2, half of 4 × 5 × 6, or 60 can be taken as the lowest common multiple and 1 can be added to this to give 61 (61p in the context of the problem).

Next step: Invite the children to include another line to the problem which reads: *If I share my money between seven people there is one penny left over.* What is the smallest amount of money (greater than £1) which satisfies this requirement?

Learning objectives
(Y5) Use/apply strand: Solve one- and two-step problems involving whole numbers and decimals and all four operations, choosing and using appropriate calculation strategies.
(Y5) Calculate strand: Extend mental methods for whole-number calculations.

11 Last one loses

Thinking skill: Reasoning about number and pattern.

What to do: Explain to the children that this is a game of planning and logic. They may take one, two or three cubes from a pile of 20. Their opponent then does the same. The player to take the final cube loses.

Probing questions: Is it better to go first or second? Is there a winning strategy?

Learning objective
(Y5) Use/apply strand: Represent a puzzle or problem by identifying and recording the information or calculations needed to solve it; find possible solutions and confirm them in the context of the problem.

Outcomes: The children should play the game a number of times to gain a feel for it. To win they need to realise that it is possible to control the total number of cubes in a combined move. The sum of the cubes taken by two players needs to be four. (If you take one, I take three, and so on). This way going second allows you to force your opponent onto the sequence 20, 16, 12, 8, 4. You then take three and leave them with one. You can win by going first if your opponent does not know the sequence.

Next step: Alter the number of cubes you begin with, or the number of cubes that can be taken at a time. How does this alter your strategy?

12 No change from a pound

Thinking skill: Reasoning about number in the context of money.

What to do: You may need to explain the problem to the children and to clarify what coins are involved. The children can make use of 1p, 2p, 5p, 10p, 20p and 50p. It may help them to have real money to work with.

Probing questions: How can you approach the problem systematically? How can you be sure you have the solution?

Outcomes: A good way to approach this problem is to realise that coins come in a sequence of 1, 2, 5, 10, 20, 50 and that the last three are simply ten times the first three. Another realisation might be that you are better off not using the 1p and 10p coins. We should use as many of the other coins as we can start with 50p + 20p + 20p + 20p + 20p. This gives us £1.30 already. We can add to this with 5p and the 4 × 2p, making £1.43 in all.

Next step: Investigate what happens if you are trying to find the largest amount you can have but not make £2. There are no £1 coins involved. Is the solution simply £1 more than the first or is it more complex?

Learning objective
(Y6) Use/apply strand:
Tabulate systematically the information in a problem or puzzle; identify and record the steps or calculations needed to solve it, using symbols where appropriate; interpret solutions in the original context and check their accuracy.

13 Diagonal sums

Thinking skill: Reasoning about number and pattern.

What to do: The children may need prompting to observe that one diagonal is always one more than the other. Invite them to test this on other diagonals on a larger grid. If you invite them to explain do not expect very precise answers.

Probing questions: Which diagonal has the higher total? What is the relationship between the numbers on adjacent rows (or columns) of a grid?

Outcomes: The children may recognise quite quickly that one diagonal is one more than another. Explaining why is quite demanding with or without algebra. If we let the column heading of one number to be a and the corresponding row heading be b, then the adjacent numbers are $a + 1$ and $b + 1$. The four numbers in the grid are ab, $ab + a$, $ab + b$ and $(a + 1)(b + 1)$. The last item is the same as $ab + a + b + 1$. When the correct pairs of items are added we can see that one pair comes to one more than the other.

Next step: Extend the activity by adding the two diagonals of a three by three grid of adjacent squares.

Learning objective:
(Y5) Use/apply strand:
Represent a puzzle or problem by identifying and recording the information or calculations needed to solve it; find possible solutions and confirm them in the context of the problem.

14 Right-angled puzzle

Thinking skill: Visualising shape and pattern.

What to do: Make sure the children appreciate that they must join their shapes together edge to edge. There can be no overlaps and the long edge of a triangle cannot be joined to a short edge. Give them squared paper on which to record their shapes.

Learning objective
(Y5) Use/apply strand:
Describe, identify and visualise parallel and perpendicular edges or faces and use these properties to classify 2D shapes.

Probing questions: How can you check for duplicate shapes which have been reflected or rotated? How can you be sure you have found them all?

Outcomes: Many of the quadrilaterals are possible. For example, you can make a square, (a non-square) rectangle, a rhombus or a trapezium.

Next step: You can classify these shapes into those with no line symmetry, one line of symmetry and four lines of symmetry. Very able children may be able to explain why you cannot have three lines of symmetry.

Learning objectives
(Y5) Use/apply strand: Represent a puzzle or problem by identifying and recording the information or calculations needed to solve it; find possible solutions and confirm them in the context of the problem.
(Y6) Data strand: Describe and predict outcomes from data using the language of chance or likelihood.

15 Dice with a difference

Thinking skill: Reasoning about number and pattern.

What to do: Explain to the children that they are doing an experiment with two dice. Make sure they understand the idea of finding the difference between the two numbers produced when the dice are thrown. Encourage them to discuss the likely results before engaging in the experiments.

Probing questions: What is the largest difference you can get? Is a difference of five very likely? Why not?

Outcomes: The practical experiment should yield convincing results that the most likely result is one. The theoretical calculation based on the grid will produce ten values of one in a table of 36.

Next step: You could invite the children to explore the product of the two numbers. Are there any values which are more likely to occur than others?

Learning objective
(Y6) Calculate strand: Use approximations, inverse operations and tests of divisibility to estimate and check results.

16 Think of a number

Thinking skill: Reasoning about number and pattern.

What to do: The children can engage with the problem at once by trying it out with numbers of their own choosing. It can be used as a trick with a large group, each of whom thinks of their own number.

Probing questions: Can you see what each step is doing to the number? How are inverses used to produce the result that you want?

Outcomes: The children need to recognise that the trick works because of the use of inverses. First of all the number is doubled, later a halving operation is used. The addition of 10, allows the value of 5 to remain after halving since the 10 is also halved.

Next step: Make a more difficult puzzle. Multiplying by 3 or squaring would be more demanding and make it difficult for others to know how the trick works.

Learning objectives
(Y5) Use/apply strand: Use sequences to scale numbers up or down; solve problems involving proportions of quantities.
(Y6) Shape strand: Make and draw shapes with increasing accuracy and apply knowledge of their properties.

17 Paper folding

Thinking skills: Reasoning about number, shape and size.

What to do: Allow children to fold a piece of 'A' sized paper in half and to realise that it is the same shape. The ratio of height to width is always the same with 'A' sizes. No other sizing method has this property.

Probing questions: Is there a quick way to calculate the number of smaller pieces of paper which can be cut from a larger one?

Outcomes: The children may notice that the 'A' sizes produce a sequence of powers of 2. (They probably won't use that term.) To calculate the number of sheets which can be cut simply multiply together the number of twos in the 'A' size. For example you can get 16 A4 pages from A0 as $2 \times 2 \times 2 \times 2 = 16$. For A6, or postcard size, we multiply together six twos to give 64.

18 The missing square

Thinking skill: Reasoning about shape.

What to do: Explain to the children that they need to cut out the puzzle on the page very carefully. It makes a better puzzle if it can be drawn much larger on card. The pieces are reassembled to make a rectangle which seems to have a larger area. The problem is to discover how this has happened.

Probing questions: What has happened to make you believe there is an extra square?

Outcomes: Many children will find it hard to believe and will spend some time arranging and rearranging the pieces. They need to be cut carefully for them to spot the problem. The 13 by 5 rectangle has a long thin hole in it, equivalent to one square in area. A more sophisticated argument can be made by looking at the slope of the line through the rectangle. It changes from $3/8$ to $2/5$. The difference is hard to spot.

Next step: Suggest to the children that they make a large colourful copy and laminate it.

Learning objectives

(Y5) Use/apply strand: Use sequences to scale numbers up or down; solve problems involving proportions of quantities.
(Y6) Shape strand: Make and draw shapes with increasing accuracy and apply knowledge of their properties.

19 Hidden shapes

Thinking skill: Reasoning about shape.

What to do: The children use the restrictions of the grid to explore squares and right-angled triangles. The aim is to encourage them to use the grid more flexibly. They will need access to dotty paper for recording.

Probing questions: Can you find squares by joining dots in an unusual way? Can you find right-angled triangles which do not have horizontal bases?

Outcomes: Squares – The children are likely to find straightforward squares first. Three of them are fairly clear based on the normal orientation of the grid. However, some children will find it a challenge to spot the other two. Right-angled triangles – Several of the right-angled triangles which are along the horizontal or vertical lines of the grid are readily seen. However, there are some which are in an unusual orientation.

Next step: Explain why you cannot make an equilateral triangle on this grid. Extend the search for squares to include all rectangles.

Learning objective

(Y5) Shape strand: Identify, visualise and describe properties of triangles and regular polygons; use knowledge of properties to draw 2D shapes.

20 Find the fruit

Thinking skills: Reasoning and logic.

What to do: Explain that this is not a trick question but one of logic and reasoning. It may help to model the problem with some boxes and cubes to represent the fruit.

Probing questions: Does it matter which box you open? Is there any useful information in the instructions?

Outcomes: The solution lies in opening the box marked 'Apples and Oranges'. You know that it contains a single sort of fruit as all the labels are wrong. If the fruit removed is an apple then move the 'Apples' label to this box, move the 'Oranges' label to the 'Apples' box and move the 'Apples and Oranges' label to the 'Oranges ' box. There is no solution you can be sure of if you open one of the other boxes.

Next step: Explain why you are certain you have found a solution.

Learning objectives

(Y5) Use/apply strand: Explain reasoning using diagrams, and text.
(Y5) Use/apply strand: Represent a puzzle or problem by identifying and recording the information needed to solve it; find possible solutions and confirm them in the context of the problem.

1: Factors

- Find a two-digit number that has 1, 2, 3, 4, 5 and 6 as factors.
- Explain why there is only one two-digit number with this property.

- Find a three-digit number that has 1, 2, 3, 4, 5, 6 and 7 as factors.
- Find all the three-digit numbers with this property.

2: Domino squares

- Here is a square of four dominoes. They are laid out so that each domino joins to one with the same number of spots on it.

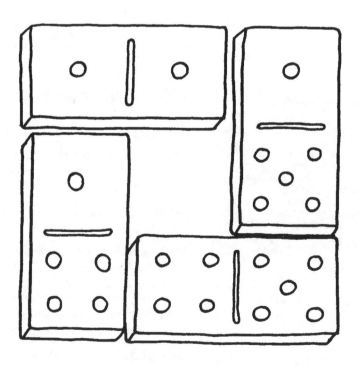

- Use all 28 dominoes from a full set to make seven squares. Lay the seven squares out together in a row.

PHOTOCOPIABLE **SCHOLASTIC**
www.scholastic.co.uk

3: How many dominoes?

You will need a full set of dominoes.

◧ Lay the set out in a
systematic way so that you
can check that you have a full set.

◧ You should have 28 different dominoes. This set is called a double-six set as
the domino with the most spots is double six.

◧ Use your layout to help you to calculate the number of dominoes in a double-
nine set.

What about a double-twelve set?

◧ I have a special set of dominoes. There are 66 dominoes in the set. What is
the largest domino? Explain how you know.

- -

4: Arithmagon investigation

◧ An arithmagon is a triangular arrangement of numbers. The ones at the
corners of the triangle add up to the number between them.

◧ Here is an arithmagon
made from the numbers
1, 2, 3, 4, 5, 6.

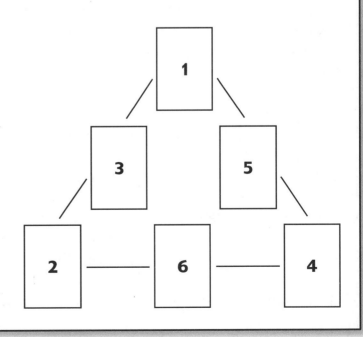

◧ Use just one set of
number cards to make as
many different
arithmagons as you can.

◧ How can you be sure
that you have found them
all?

5: Target numbers

■ Here you can see the number cards 1, 2, 3, 4, and 5 and the symbols +, – and × have been used to make a mathematical statement with the answer of 17.

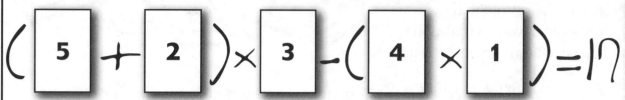

$$(5 + 2) \times 3 - (4 \times 1) = 17$$

■ Brackets have also been used to make sure that the 3 + 2 is carried out first.

■ Make statements with answers for each of the numbers between 1 and 20. You may use brackets.

■ You must use all five digits each time, but only once.

■ You can use the symbols as often as you wish.

✂ ---

6: 1001 calculations

You will need a calculator and a partner.

■ Give your partner a calculator and ask them to write down a three-digit number, such as 347. Ask them to create a six-digit number from it by repeating the first three digits. This example would give 347 347. They must not show you the number.

■ Tell them that you are going to perform some lighting fast calculations. Here is what to do.

■ Ask them to divide their six-digit number by 7. Now ask them to divide their result by 11. Then ask them to divide the result by their original number.

■ After a short pause, tell them that the answer is 13.

■ Can you discover how this calculation feat works?

7: How old is Gran?

◀ A girl, her mother and her grandmother have a combined age of 90 years.

◀ The mother is half the age of the grandmother.

◀ The girl is one third the age of the mother.

◀ How old is the grandmother?

◀ The girl's father said, "I am the average age of all of you." How can you work out his age quickly?

8: Leaky tank

◀ A large tank can be filled with water from two taps, A and B.

◀ If only tap A is used, the tank takes one hour to fill.

◀ If only tap B is used, it takes half an hour to fill.

◀ How long does it take to fill the tank if both taps are used?

◀ If the tank has a leak which can empty it in two hours, how long does it take to fill with both taps now?

9: Make 15

This is a short game for two or three players.
◼ Take one set of 1–9 digit cards and place them face up on a table.
◼ One player starts and takes a card.
◼ The next player takes a card from those remaining.
◼ Play continues until one player has cards that total 15.

Devise a winning strategy to this game.

◼ Is it better to start or to go second?

◼ Is there one card that is better than the others?

10: One penny left over

I have less than a pound in my pocket.
◼ If I share my money between two people, there is one penny left over.
◼ If I share my money between three people, there is one penny left over.
◼ If I share my money between four people, there is one penny left over.
◼ If I share my money between five people, there is one penny left over.
◼ If I share my money between six people, there is one penny left over.

How much money do I have?

11: Last one loses

This is a game for two players.

Rules:
- Place 20 cubes or counters in a pile.
- Each player is allowed to take one, two or three cubes from the pile.
- The person who takes the last cube loses.

12: No change from a pound

- I have a lot of coins in my pocket.
- Each one is less than a pound.
- I cannot make an exact total of £1 with them.

- What is the largest amount of money I could have but not be able to exchange some of the coins for exactly a pound?

13: Diagonal sums

You will need a multiplication grid.

◼ Choose four numbers that make a square in the grid. On the small multiplication grid below, the numbers 12, 16, 15, and 20 have been selected. Add the two numbers along one diagonal and the two numbers along the other diagonal.

◼ What do you notice?

◼ Check your ideas by trying several other groups of four numbers.

◼ Can you explain your observations?

	2	3	4	5	6	7	8
2	4	6	8	10	12	14	16
3	6	9	12	15	18	21	24
4	8	12	16	20	24	28	32
5	10	15	20	25	30	35	40
6	12	18	24	30	36	42	48
7	14	21	28	35	42	49	56
8	16	24	32	40	48	56	64

14: Right-angled puzzle

◼ Take two squares and cut them in half along their diagonals. You have made four congruent, right-angled triangles.

◼ Make as many different shapes as you can, using all four of these triangles together.

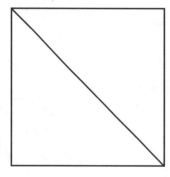

◼ You must join triangles edge to edge with no overlaps.

◼ How many shapes can you name?

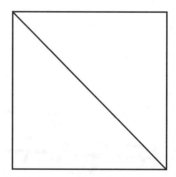

15: Dice with a difference

You need two ordinary dice.
Thought experiment
◀ Think about throwing the two dice and finding the difference between the two numbers. What number do you think will be the most likely difference?
Try to explain why.

	1	2	3	4	5	6
1						
2						
3						
4						
5						
6						

Practical experiment
◀ Throw the two dice 36 times and record the results in a tally chart.
◀ Decide what the most likely result is from your chart.

Theoretical calculation
◀ Use the grid above to record all the possible differences between the values on the two dice. Think about how these results fit with your original thoughts and with the experiment above.

16: Think of a number

Follow this sequence of steps.

◀ Think of a number between one and ten.
    Double your number.
        Add ten.
            Halve your number.
                Take away the number you first thought of.

Your answer should be five.

Why is the answer always five?

◀ Does this work if you start with a larger number?

◀ Can you make a series of similar questions for which the answer is always eight?

17: Paper folding

■ Paper often comes in sizes such as A4 and A3. The number is a measure of its size.

■ As the number reduces by 1, the paper doubles in size. A3 is double the size of A4.

■ As the number increases by 1, the paper halves in size. Fold a piece of A4 paper in half to produce A5.

■ A0 is the largest paper normally available. How many sheets of A4 can you get from a sheet of A0?

■ Lay out some A4 sheets of paper to cover the size you think an A0 sheet will be.

■ A0 paper is one square metre in area. Use this to work out the area of a sheet of A4. Measure a sheet, and use a calculator to check.

■ A6 is a size that can be used for postcards. How many postcards can be cut from a piece of A0 card?

18: The missing square

◧ Cut out the four pieces below very carefully. Alternatively, draw them accurately but larger onto a piece of squared paper.

◧ These pieces form an 8 × 8 square that has an area of 64.

◧ Rearrange the pieces to make a 13 × 5 rectangle, with an area of 65.

◧ Can you explain where the extra square has come from?

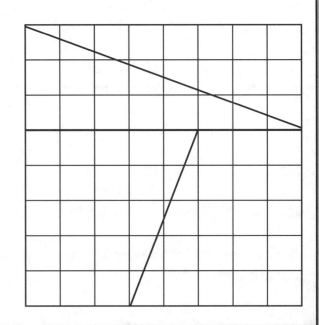

19: Hidden shapes

■ You will need a piece of square dotty paper to record your results.

■ You are only allowed to use 16 dots arranged in a square. By joining dots find:

1 Five different-sized squares.
2 Eight different-sized right-angled triangles.

· · · ·

· · · ·

· · · ·

· · · ·

20: Find the fruit

There are three boxes of fruit. One box contains apples, one contains oranges and one an equal mixture of apples and oranges.

Sadly all of the labels are wrong.

■ You are allowed to open one box and without looking, put your hand in and take one fruit out.

■ After that you have to correct all of the labels.

■ Which box do you open?

■ What do you do with the information?

Tricky towers

Activity introduction

● Give each child some linking cubes and ask them to build a tower with the following rules. Read the rules as a set of clues, one at a time; display them on the board for the children to see.

The tower has five cubes and five colours.
There is a red cube on top of a yellow one.
There is a white cube below a blue one.
There is a green cube in the middle.

● Ask the children to display their towers. If they are all the same, ask them if they can be sure this is the only tower which can be built with these clues. If necessary, produce two ready-made towers and ask them to confirm that they both fit the clues. The towers, from top to bottom, are: red, yellow, green, blue and white; blue, white, green, red, yellow.

● Invite a debate about the need for additional clues to make sure that only one tower fits them all. Challenge the children to offer such a clue. Explain that they should consider a clue which eliminates one of the towers. They will probably need some time to discuss this. Invite them to check carefully that their new clue does what is intended.

Activity development

● Provide each child with photocopiable page 29. The activity offers sets of clues similar to those in the introduction. However, the clues become increasingly demanding. The words for all of the clues have been chosen with care.

● Sometimes it is clear that only one cube of a particular colour is needed. For example, 'the red cube is in the middle' is an unambiguous statement. If, however, the clue says 'a red cube is in the middle', then there may be more than one red cube.

Solution

(Top to bottom) Four-cube tower: blue, red, yellow, white.
Five-cube tower: yellow, black, red, green, red.
Seven-cube tower: There is more than one possible solution. For example 1) black, blue, yellow, blue, purple, purple, green; 2) yellow, blue, purple, green, black, black, blue.

Review

● Invite the children to share their solutions and check as a group that any tower offered fits all of the clues.

● If there is time, ask for any sets of clues which the children have created and allow the class or group to create the tower. It is usually best if the clues can be written down as it is very difficult to hold all of the information in the head.

Learning objectives
(Y6) Use/apply strand:
Explain reasoning and conclusions, using symbols where appropriate.

Expected prior knowledge
● Appreciate that logical statements need to be precise and unambiguous.
● Recognise that logical problems need to be approached with care.

You will need
Linking cubes (set of red, yellow, green, blue and white per child plus two sets for demonstration); photocopiable page 29 (one per child); more linking cubes in additional colours.

Key vocabulary
logical, reasoning, precise

Next steps
● A demanding task is to invite children to make a 2 × 2 × 2 cube with eight of the linking cubes, in a variety of colours. They then devise clues which will allow a partner to make the same cube as them. They will need to be advised to avoid unhelpful language, such as 'next to', and to be very precise and unambiguous.

Tricky towers

You will need a variety of coloured cubes, including red, yellow, green, orange, purple, white, blue and black.

Four cubes are joined to make a tower.
◀ Use these clues to create the tower.
The red cube is not at the top.
The white cube is below the yellow one.
The blue cube is not touching the yellow one.
The yellow cube touches two other cubes.

Another tower is made from five cubes.
◀ Use these clues to create the tower.
One colour appears twice.
The black cube is near the top.
The yellow cube is not in the middle.
The green cube is between the two cubes of the same colour.
There is a red cube in the middle.

This puzzle is more difficult.
◀ Read the words in each of these clues very carefully and create the tower.
A blue cube touches both a yellow one and a purple one.
A black cube is just above a blue one.
A green cube is just below a purple one.
Five colours are needed to make the tower.
A blue cube and a green cube have two the same colour between them.
There is only one yellow cube.

◀ Make up a tricky tower puzzle of your own and give it to a partner to solve.

PHOTOCOPIABLE   ⬛ 29

Intersecting loops (1)

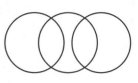

Learning objectives
(Y5) Use/apply strand:
Solve one- and two-step
problems involving whole
numbers.
(Y5) Use/apply strand:
Explain reasoning using
diagrams; refine ways of
recording using images and
symbols.

**Expected prior
knowledge**
● Show confidence at
working through a puzzle
independently.
● Be systematic in their
approach.
● Show knowledge of
logical reasoning.

You will need
Photocopiable page 31 (one
per child/pair); 18 counters
or small cubes.

Key vocabulary
Venn diagram

Brainteaser link
10. One penny left over

Activity introduction

● Explain that this activity is about reasoning
logically. Draw three intersecting loops like those
shown on the right. Invite the children to make a
large copy on paper.

● Tell the children they must arrange ten counters so that there are
exactly five counters in each loop, and none left over. Allow the children
time to explore the problem and to discuss it. Make sure that they
understand that there are only three loops and that they do not become
confused by the other regions.

● This problem has three distinct solutions. Once all three solutions
have been found ask the children what methods they used

Activity development

● Give each child or pair a copy of photocopiable page 31. This develops
the activity by using more counters. It also offers the children space to
record their results.

● Using the diagram below as a guide, here are some solutions using
18 counters. The number in the first column is the total for each loop.
Children may have a mathematically identical solution but with the
numbers in the reverse order.

	A	B	C	D	E
6	6	0	6	0	6
7	5	2	4	1	6
8	5	3	2	3	5
8	6	2	2	4	4
8	7	1	2	5	3
9	4	5	0	4	5
9	1	8	0	8	1

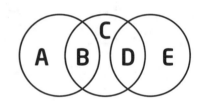

● Discuss the symmetry possibilities of all of the solutions. Explain why
they are mathematically identical.

Review

● Briefly check that the solutions to the first part of the activity are
correct. The second part is more demanding and more open-ended in
approach. It is possible to produce a total of six or seven in only one way
(see table above). A total of eight can be produced in three distinct
ways. There are other ways to produce a total of nine if you leave region
C empty.

Next steps
● Extend the activity by adding another loop, which intersects in the
same way as the others. Set the number of counters between 12 and
20, and set problems such as getting the same number of counters in
each loop. Where a solution is impossible, invite the children to explain
why.
● The activity, Lesson 3 Intersecting Loops (2), requires the children to
work with additional properties and involves three mutually
intersecting loops, in a Venn diagram.

Name _____

Intersecting loops (1)

In this activity you need to use exactly 12 counters.

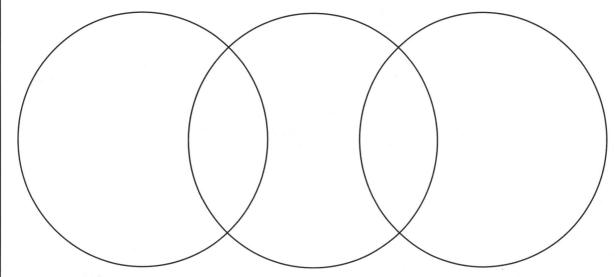

■ Arrange them so that each circular loop has exactly five counters inside it with no counters left over. One way is shown on the right. Find another way to arrange five counters in each loop.

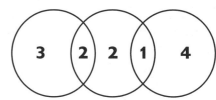

Record your solution here:

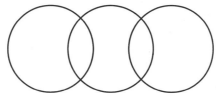

■ Find four different ways to arrange six counters in each loop with none left over.

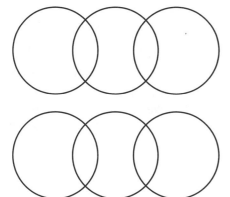

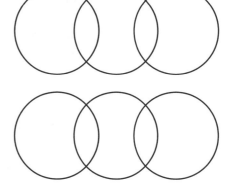

■ Explore all the different totals that are possible with exactly 18 counters. You can leave some of the intersecting regions empty. Record them on the back of this sheet. You might like to use a two pence piece to help you draw the loops.

Intersecting loops (2)

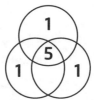

Activity introduction
● Explain that this activity is about reasoning logically. Draw three intersecting loops like those shown on the right, but leave out the numbers. Invite the children to make a large copy on paper.
● Tell the children they must arrange eight counters so that there are exactly six counters in each loop, and none left over. Allow the children time to explore the problem and to discuss it. Make sure that they understand that there are only three loops and that they do not become confused by the other regions. One of the solutions is shown above. Another has four 2s placed symmetrically about the centre. Other solutions are difficult to find and could be left as a challenge.

Activity development
● Give each child or pair a copy of photocopiable page 33. This develops the activity by using ten counters. It also offers the children space to record their results.
● Encourage them to extend the activity by trying to find more solutions than those asked for.
● The diagram below shows some solutions using ten counters. The number in the first column is the total for each loop. Children may have a mathematically identical solution but with the numbers in a different order. There are many other solutions.
● Invite the children to recognise any symmetries which are to be found in solutions. In particular, they should note those that can be used to help with solutions.

	A	B	C	D	E	F	G
4	3	0	1	0	3	0	3
5	2	1	1	1	2	1	2
6	1	2	1	2	1	2	1
7	0	3	1	3	0	3	0
8	0	2	4	2	0	2	0
9	0	1	7	1	0	1	0
10	0	0	10	0	0	0	0

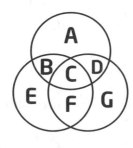

Review
● Briefly check that the solutions to the first two parts of the activity are correct. The final part is more demanding and more open-ended in approach. It is possible for loops to have any total from four to ten. Many of these can be made in more than one way. Discuss any symmetrical properties that have allowed solutions to be found more readily.

Next steps
● A useful homework or extension task is to ask the children to find all the possible ways for a given total, and to explain how they know that they have them all.
For example: *If I have 15 counters, and I want to arrange the same number in each loop, what solutions are possible?* The most able learners may be able to generalise this for *n* counters.

Intersecting loops (2)

◼ Arrange all ten of your counters so that each circular loop has exactly four counters inside it. Record your results below.

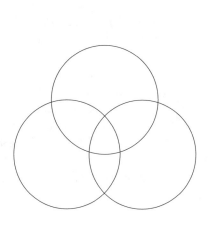

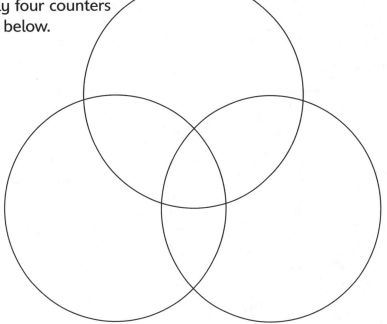

◼ Can you find three different ways to arrange all ten counters so that there are five in each loop?

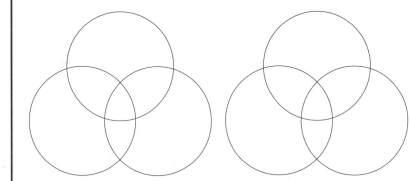

◼ Find and record as many different ways as you can to make each loop have six, seven, eight, nine or ten counters in each loop. Use the back of this sheet to continue your recording. You may like to use a 2p piece to help you draw the loops.

Fraction squeeze

Activity introduction

Learning objectives
(Y5) Counting strand:
Express a smaller whole number as a fraction of a larger one; relate fractions to their decimal representations.
(Y6/Y7) Counting strand:
Order a set of fractions by converting them to decimals.

Expected prior knowledge
● Some secure knowledge of fractions less than one (in particular this activity should come after work on equivalent fractions).
● Practice in using a calculator to compare the decimal equivalents of fractions.

You will need
Four sets of 1-9 digit cards (per pair); photocopiable page 35; calculators; coloured pencils.

Key vocabulary
numerator, denominator, equivalent

● Give each pair of children a set of 1-9 digit cards. Keep a set for yourself. Select the cards 1, 2, 3 and 4. Use them to make the fractions ½ and ¾. Ask each child to produce a fraction that is between these two fractions. Allow pairs time to discuss this. Remind them that they have a set of cards between them to use to create and display their fraction. (Possible fractions: $2/3$, $4/7$ and $5/8$.)

● Ask the children how they know that their fraction is between ½ and ¾. Encourage an explanation that uses equivalent fractions. For example, $6/8$ is equivalent to $3/4$ and $4/8$ is equivalent to ½, $5/8$ must be between the two.

● Many fractions that satisfy the condition, such as $5/7$, are too difficult for most to do without a calculator. However, encourage imaginative insightful answers as children gain confidence, if they have a feel for the size of fractions. For example, $5/7$ is a little larger than $5/8$. It is also $2/7$ less than one, whereas $3/4$ is equivalent to $6/8$ and is therefore $2/8$ less than one. From this we can deduce that $5/7$ is a little less than $3/4$.

● Repeat the exercise with the fractions $2/3$ and $4/5$. Give children time to discuss and test their ideas with a calculator.

Activity development

● Hand out copies of photocopiable page 35 to each pair. Ensure that children fully understand the rules of the game.

● Give out the other sets of number cards (two sets of 1-9 digit cards each, four sets per pair). Remind them that they need to manage their sets so that they do not become mixed up. Each player should place their cards face up in front of them so they can see both their own and their opponent's cards.

● Coloured circles are used to distinguish one player from another, and a player may mark a circle at the same point as their opponent. You will need several copies of the sheet for each player, a fresh sheet for each game.

Review

● Ask the children if there are any good fractions to choose early on in order to gain an advantage. Ask them how they managed their cards knowing that they had two sets of cards each. If they used the calculator to explore their next move, invite them to share strategies. This is the sort of game in which children get noticeably better after playing a few times. Once they are proficient, have the whole group cooperate against you.

Next steps
● Invite the children to explore the decimal equivalent of the set of fractions $1/7$, $2/7$, $3/7$, $4/7$, $5/7$ and $6/7$. They record any patterns they see in the sequence of numbers. The fraction $1/7$ (and each of the others) produces a recurring decimal. $1/7 = 0.142857142857$. The most able may be encouraged to explore other recurring decimals such as $1/13$ or $1/17$.

Fraction squeeze

Player two

Place your number cards here.

Place your number cards here.

■ This is a game for two players. Each player needs two sets of 1–9 digit cards, a calculator and a coloured pencil.

■ Take turns to take two of your digit cards and make a fraction. Convert the fraction into a decimal and mark a coloured circle on the number line in the correct place.

■ Place the cards to one side as you cannot use them again.

The winner is the first person to mark three coloured circles on the number line without an opponent's circle between them.

Player one

Place your number cards here.

Place your number cards here.

0   0.1   0.2   0.3   0.4   0.5   0.6   0.7   0.8   0.9   1.0

Ordering fractions

Activity introduction

- Give each pair of a set of 1-9 digit cards. Keep a set for yourself. Select the cards 3 and 4 and make the fraction ¾. Ask each child to produce a fraction that is smaller than yours. Allow them time to discuss this with their partners. Remind them that they have a set of cards between them to use to create and display their fraction. Possible pairings of fractions include, $^2/_3$ and $^4/_7$, $^2/_5$ and $^3/_8$, and so on.
- Ask the children how they know that their fractions are all less than ¾. Encourage an explanation that uses equivalent fractions. If there is dispute or doubt, then use a calculator. However, the activity should be used to encourage children to gain a greater feel for the size of a fraction without the use of a calculator.
- Repeat the exercise using the fraction ½. Tell the children that this time they must resolve any disputes without the calculator.

Activity development

- Hand out a copy of photocopiable page 37 to each pair and explain the rules of the game.
- The pairs have one set of 1-9 digit cards between them. These should be shuffled and placed face down. Each player in turn takes a card and places it in one of their boxes. The card cannot be moved once placed.
- After eight cards are taken (and one is left in the pile) the children should discuss the fractions they have formed. The aim of the game is that the one on the left should be smaller than the one on the right. Disputes can be resolved with a calculator. Children score one point if the fraction on the left is smaller. Fractions that are equal do not score. The winner is the first child to score five points.

Review

- Ask the children for strategies that allow them to decide which of the two fractions is the larger. Some children may be comfortable with finding and using common denominators and others may not. However, it is a good idea to avoid the procedural use of common denominators in favour of a discussion about equivalent fractions. Such a discussion will involve comparing fractions whose denominators are equal, but the focus will be on the equivalence, and not on a rule to make denominators equal.

Learning objectives
(Y5) Counting strand:
Express a smaller whole number as a fraction of a larger one; relate fractions to their decimal representations.
(Y6/Y7) Counting strand:
Order a set of fractions by converting them to decimals.

Expected prior knowledge
- Secure knowledge of fractions less than one (in particular this activity should come after work on equivalent fractions).
- Use a calculator to compare the decimal equivalents of fractions.

You will need
Photocopiable page 37; calculator; set of 1-9 digit cards per pair.

Key vocabulary
numerator, denominator, equivalent

Next steps
- A more demanding variation on the game can be played where a player can place a number card on any vacant space. This means that they can place a card on an opponent's side of the board in order to make it harder (or impossible) for them to win. Another extension can be managed by the players themselves in which they agree to play with one of the cards missing. For example, they could explore what happens when the digit 1 is removed from the game.

Name _____

Ordering fractions

Player two

Player one

- This is a game for two players. You will need a set of 1–9 digit cards and a calculator.
- Each player, in turn, takes the next digit card from the pile and places it in one of their boxes until eight cards are placed. Once placed, cards cannot be moved.
- The aim of the game is to create two fractions, but the one on the left must be less than the one on the right. Use a calculator to check your fractions if necessary.
- Score one point when the fraction on the left is smaller. Equal fractions do not score. The winner is the first one to five points.

Pipes

Learning objectives
(Y5) Use/apply strand:
Solve one- and two-step problems involving whole numbers and decimals and all four operations, choosing and using appropriate calculation strategies.
(Y5) Counting strand:
Count from any given number in whole-number and decimal steps.
(Y5) Knowledge strand:
Identify pairs of factors of two-digit whole numbers and find common multiples.

Expected prior knowledge
● Work with factors and multiples and some understanding of the relationship between them.

You will need
Photocopiable page 39 (one per pair).

Key vocabulary
factor, multiple, ('pipe run' is used to refer to a length of pipe made up from smaller lengths)

Brainteaser link
1. Factors

Activity introduction
● Tell the children that it has been suggested that 1p coins are to be abolished. Ask them what that will mean for the prices of objects. Allow them time to discuss the problem as they may have a variety of different perspectives to offer.
● Draw their attention to the fact that nothing could be priced as 1p or 3p. (All other values are possible.)
● Ask them how they would make 11p or 13p.
● Ask them to find two different ways to make 17p.
● Ask: *What is the smallest amount that can be made in exactly three different ways?* Give them a little time to consider their answer and to check for other possibilities. The answer is 10p, which can be made as 2 × 5p, 1 × 10p or 5 × 2p.
● Some children may offer larger values such as 22p, which can be made in four different ways. Follow this up by asking for the smallest amount which can be made in four different ways.

Activity development
● Hand out and introduce photocopiable page 39 to the children. Explain what a pipe run is (a length of pipe made up from smaller lengths). You may want to reiterate the connections between this and the introductory activity.
● Make sure the children understand the table. They need to realise that the numbers along the top and down the side refer to the number of lengths of pipe used and not to the lengths of the pipes themselves.
● Go through an entry in the table with the group, so they are clear about the objectives.
● Identify where the children write their explanations. There is room on the page to complete the table but not to write notes of explanation.

Review
● A significant part of the activity is concerned with explaining that every pipe run over 23m is possible. Ask a few children to prepare an explanation before the review begins, to give them time to rehearse what they want to say.
● If the children are struggling with an explanation, then draw their attention to the last digit in the entries in the table. Every possible last digit (0–9) can be seen. In addition, we can always add 10m by adding on two 5m pipes. These two observations should allow them to see that we can construct any pipe over 23m.

Next steps
● Return to the money problem tackled in the introduction and ask the children to discuss why nearly every currency uses decimal units. Ask them to explain why every currency uses 1, 2, 5 and 10 for the 'steps' in its currency.
● You might also ask them to find some advantages of non-decimal currencies. At the time of writing, there is a good article on Wikipedia at **http://en.wikipedia.org/wiki/non-decimal_currencies**

Pipes

🪣 A factory makes large water pipes. They only make them in 5m and 7m lengths. Pipe runs are long lengths of pipe made up from any mixture of 5m and 7m pipes.

🪣 How could you make a pipe run of 17m? _____

_____

🪣 Find two ways to make a pipe run of 42m. _____

_____

🪣 Explain why you cannot make a pipe run of 16m. _____

_____

🪣 The company uses a table to let customers know which pipe runs can be made and which ones are impossible. Explain how the entries shown in the table below answer the first two questions above.

Number of 7m lengths

	0	**1**	**2**	**3**	**4**	**5**	**6**
0							42
1							
2		17					
3							
4							
5							
6							
7		42					

Number of 5m lengths

🪣 Complete the table. The company claims that they can make any pipe run over 23m. Explain why this claim is correct.

_____

🪣 Use your explanation to show how to make a pipe run of 103m.

Sequences (1)

Activity introduction

● Make sure that the children understand the idea of a sequence. A sequence can be defined as a list of numbers, in which each number is related to its neighbour by a simple rule. All of the sequences here have equal gaps between the numbers and start with a whole number.

● Rehearse the activity with a few simple examples. If possible, represent these sequences as jumps along a number line. The number line is an important model to help the children understand sequences.

● Ask the children for the next two numbers in each of the sequences on the right. The answers are given in brackets after each sequence.

2, 4, 6, 8 _, _ (10, 12)
7, 10, 13, 16 _, _ (19, 22)
20, 16, 12, 8 _, _ (4, 0)
7, 11, 15 _, _ (19, 23)

Activity development

● Continue by explaining that if numbers are missing from the middle of a sequence, you must use reasoning to work out what the numbers should be. Ask the children for the missing numbers in each of the sequences below. The answers are given in brackets after each sequence.

3, _, _, 12 (6, 9)
4, _, _, 19 (9, 14)
5, _, _, _, 17 (8, 11, 14)

● Hand out copies of photocopiable page 41, which asks the children to fill in gaps in sequences. The first four sequences are straightforward, and the size of the gaps can be calculated by finding the difference between any two adjacent terms. For the remainder, the sizes of gaps need to be calculated. Explain the following strategy to the children as a tool to use in their calculation.

● To calculate the size of the gaps between numbers in a sequence, take whatever gap or difference is available and divide it by the number of jumps. For example, the fifth question shows the sequence: 12, _, _, _, _, _, 30. In this sequence, the overall gap is 18 (30–12) and there are six jumps. Therefore each of the jumps is 18 ÷ 6 = 3.

Solutions (to the second section)

5, 10, 15, 20, 25, 30, 35, 40
5, 12, 19, 26, 33, 40
8, 12, 16, 20, 24, 28, 32, 36, 40
4, 13, 22, 31, 40

7, 18, 29, 40
55, 52, 49, 46, 43, 40
72, 64, 56, 48, 40

Review

● Invite the children to give their solutions and explain how each answer was calculated. If there is time, use one of the sequences produced with the remainder of the class. It may be worth discussing the rule that each child has used before the sequence is presented.

Next steps

● Make a few towers eight or ten bricks high from coloured linking cubes. Make sure there is a repeating pattern evident, such as red, white, blue, blue, red, white, blue, blue, and so on. Ask the children what the colour will be of cube number 100 and cube number 1000. Ask them to justify their answers.

Sequences (1)

◀ All the sequences on this page have equal gaps between each number. Sequences can start with any number.

◀ Fill in the gaps in these sequences.

1	_	5	_	_	11	13
3	_	_	15	19	_	27
_	20	_	_	_	8	5	_
_	_	_	_	_	26	30
12	_	_	_	_	_	30

◀ In each of these sequences the last number is 40. Find all the missing numbers.

5	_	_	_	_	_	_	40
5	_	_	_	_	40		
8	_	_	_	_	_	_	_	40
4	_	_	_	40			
7	_	_	40				
55	_	_	_	_	40		
72	_	_	_	40			

◀ Make some sequences of your own. Each one must start with a number below 10 and end with 30. Make your sequences into challenges to give to a partner.

Sequences (2)

Activity introduction

● A sequence can be defined as a list of numbers, in which each number is related to its neighbour by a simple rule. Make sure that the children are comfortable with sequences in which the step sizes are equal. The first few sequences in this activity have equal gaps between the numbers, but most have variable gaps.

● Explain that in the first sequence, each of the gaps is the same size.

● Present the children with the challenge to find the missing numbers in 5, _, _, _, 17. The numbers are 8, 11 and 14. Ask the children to explain how they calculated the numbers. Follow up with the sequence 3, _, _, _, _, _, 27. Invite the children to discuss different ways of solving the problem.

Activity development

● Continue by explaining that in some sequences the gaps are not all the same size. Ask the children for the next two numbers in the sequence: 1, 3, 6, 10. The numbers required are 15 and 21 as the gaps are increasing in size by one each time.

● Discuss different methods of finding the solution. One powerful method is to construct a difference table, where the gaps or differences between numbers are used to find the rule. A difference table can be set out in columns or on a number line. The number line format is shown below, with the solution for the example above filled in.

1		3		6		10		15		21
	2		3		4		5		6	
		1		1		1		1		

● Explain to the children that they need to use the pattern formed by the gaps (or by the gaps in the gaps). They can then work back from this information and complete the table and sequence.

● Continue with a difference table based on the square numbers. Use the sequence: 1, 4, 9, 16, 25, 36. Even though the children may know the answer because of their knowledge of square numbers, ask them to form a difference table like the one above. This sequence is repeated on photocopiable page 43.

● The two most difficult ones are shown below. The second of these requires an extra line before the numbers are all the same. The original sequence is the cube numbers.

-1		2		9		20		35		54		77		104
	3		7		11		15		19		23		27	
		4		4		4		4		4		4		

1		8		27		64		125		216		343
	7		19		37		61		91		127	
	12		18		24		30		36		
		6		6		6		6			

Review

● Ask the children to explain how each of the difference tables was calculated. Go over one or two of the more difficult ones from the first section to ensure that they understand the need to continue with differences between the numbers until all the numbers in a row are the same.

Next steps

● Ask the children to write down the doubling sequence 1, 2, 4, 8, 16, 32 and so on, leaving gaps between each number. Form a difference table. Ask what they notice. Explain how this table is different from those studied in the activity.

Sequences (2)

◼ The sequences on this page are all formed using simple rules.

◼ Find the rule and complete the sequences. Draw a difference table using the space beneath each sequence.

_   _   _   _   26   30   34

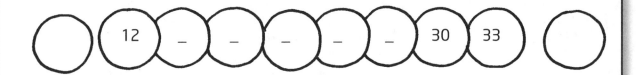

2   4   7   11   16   _   _

2   6   12   20   30   42   _   _

◼ These two sequences are very difficult. Can you work them out?

-1   2   9   20   35   54   _   _

_   8   27   64   125   216   _

Make a big difference

Learning objectives
(Y5) Use/apply strand:
Solve one- and two-step
problems involving whole
numbers.
(Y6) Knowledge strand:
Use knowledge of place
value and multiplication
facts to derive related facts.

**Expected prior
knowledge**
● Understand place value.

You will need
Photocopiable page 45; set
of 0-9 number cards (one
per child/pair).

Key vocabulary
product, difference (as
applied to calculation with
numbers)

Activity introduction

● Ask the children to select two digits from their set of 0-9 digit cards that have difference of five. Ask: *How many ways can you pick a pair of digits with a difference of five?* Discuss their responses and ensure that every child understands that the difference between two numbers is the larger number subtract the smaller.

● Ask the children to hold up two two-digit numbers with a difference of 11. With only one set of number cards each, they will need to think more carefully about this.

● Ask the children to make two two-digit numbers with the largest difference possible. Give them a little time to settle on 10 and 98.

● Ask the children for two digits with a product of six. If children hold up 4 and 2 (or 5 and 1) rather than 3 and 2, you will need to remind them that the word 'product' means multiply.

● Finally ask them to make two numbers with a product of 36.

Activity development

● Explain that the main activity requires them to make the largest possible product from a set of digits. To explore this idea, ask the children to make any product from the digits 2, 3 and 5 and to write down both the calculation and the answer.

● There are six possible products the children could make. Write down the ones made by the group and then add to them until you have all six. Ask the children to identify the largest product ($52 \times 3 = 156$ and $32 \times 5 = 160$, are both good candidates). Ask them to explain how they could know these two might be the best ones to choose to give the largest product, without working out the answer first. Encourage them to offer an explanation based on place value.

● Children use photocopiable page 45, their digit cards and a calculator.

Solutions

Set of numbers	Largest product	Smallest product	Difference
1,2,3	$3 \times 21 = 63$	$1 \times 23 = 23$	40
1,2,3,4	$41 \times 32 = 1312$	$1 \times 234 = 234$	1078
1,2,3,4,5	$52 \times 431 = 22412$	$1 \times 2345 = 2345$	20067
1,2,3,4,5,6	$631 \times 542 = 342002$	$1 \times 23456 = 23456$	318546

Review

● Explore the methods the children have used to find the largest and smallest products. The arrangement giving the largest product is surprising. Most children will believe the largest result will come from alternating the digits, rather than from a small variation of this pattern.

Next steps
● Ask the children to use the digits 1 to 8 and then 1 to 9 to check any patterns they have found in the maximum possible product. There is an additional problem for them to solve in that most calculators 'run out of space'. The display will not show all of the digits of the calculation so the children will need to be imaginative. If they use a scientific calculator, make sure they do not lose accuracy by rounding.

Make a big difference

▪ You will need a set of 1–9 digit cards and a calculator for this activity. Start with the digits 1, 2 and 3.

▪ Using all of the digits, arrange them to make two numbers that have the largest product possible.

▪ Write the arrangement and the product in the table.

▪ Arrange the same digits to make the smallest product possible and enter this in the table.

▪ Calculate the difference between these numbers.

Set of numbers	Largest product	Smallest product	Difference
1 , 2 , 3			
1 , 2 , 3 , 4			
1 , 2 , 3 , 4 , 5			
1 , 2 , 3 , 4 , 5 , 6			

▪ Describe the way you need to set out the digits to make the largest product.

_____

_____

▪ Describe the way you need to set out the digits to make the smallest product.

_____

_____

▪ Test your ideas by using the digits from 1 to 7.

_____

_____

Missing numbers

Learning objectives
(Y5) Knowledge strand:
Recall quickly multiplication facts up to 10 × 10.
(Y5) Use/apply strand:
Represent a problem by identifying and recording the calculations needed to solve it; find possible solutions and confirm them in the context of the problem.

Expected prior knowledge
● Show knowledge of multiplication tables to 10 × 10 (or preferably 12 × 12) and confidence with the multiplication grid to 20 × 20.

You will need
Photocopiable page 47 (one per child); calculators.

Key vocabulary
consecutive numbers

Brainteaser link
5. Target numbers

Activity introduction
● Draw the multiplication grid shown here on an OHP or interactive whiteboard.

×			
	24		
			40
			48

● Explain to the children that it is part of a special multiplication grid. The shaded boxes contain the numbers that are to be multiplied together. The grid does not start at 1.
● Ask: *How can we decide what the missing numbers are?*
● If more prompting is needed, then ask them for pairs of numbers that, multiplied together, make 24. One of these numbers appears in the top row and one of them appears in the left column.
● Tell them that the numbers in the shaded boxes are consecutive. Ask: *Can we use the other numbers in the grid to give us any more information?*
● If necessary, focus the children's attention on the relationship between 40 and 48. (The difference of 8 must tell us what the number is in the top row.)
● If there is time, the numbers 24 and 48 can be replaced with 21 and 45 respectively, to create another grid of similar difficulty. A more demanding grid can be created by replacing 24, 40 and 48 with 132, 169 and 182 respectively.

Activity development
● Hand out a copy of photocopiable page 47 to each child. This has four grids, the first being very straightforward and the last requiring knowledge of multiplication facts above 12 × 12. A calculator should be used for this part of the activity.
● Some children may need support to make full use of the information in the grid. Remind them of the methods used in the introduction, such as finding the difference between pairs of numbers in a grid, or that multiplication grids have consecutive numbers along the top and down the left-hand side.

Review
● Use this time to share the methods that the children used to solve the grids. For example, ask them: *Which numbers were the best to start with?* Focus much of the discussion on the final grid. This will extend the children's knowledge and confidence with multiplication facts beyond the traditional barrier of 10 × 10 (or 12 × 12).

Next steps
● Invite the children to make a grid of their own with three rows and columns of numbers. They must put in only enough numbers to allow the grid to be solved uniquely. This concept of minimal necessary information is an important one in mathematics and may need further explanation. The children can exchange their grids with a partner.

Missing numbers

■ These diagrams are small parts of special multiplication grids. The numbers in the shaded boxes are multiplied together to give the numbers in the white boxes.
■ Find all the missing numbers.

×				
		40		56
	36			63
	40		60	
		55	66	

×		
	18	21
	24	28

×			
		32	36
	35	40	
	42	48	54

■ This grid is part of a 20 × 20 multiplication grid. Can you complete it?

×				
	168		196	
	180			225
		208			256
		221			272
			252	270	

Factor trees

Learning objectives
(Y5) Knowledge strand:
Identify pairs of factors of
two-digit whole numbers
and find common multiples,
eg for 6 and 9.
(Y6) Knowledge strand:
Recognise that prime
numbers have only two
factors and identify prime
numbers less than 100; find
the prime factors of two-
digit numbers.

**Expected prior
knowledge**
● Understand and use
factors and multiples of a
number.

You will need
Photocopiable page 49 (one
for each child).

Key vocabulary
prime, prime factors,
multiple, highest common
factor

Brainteaser link
1. Factors

Activity introduction

● Ask the children to write down all of the factors of 36. Check that they have them all (1, 2, 3, 4, 6, 9, 12, 18 and 36), including 1 and 36. Repeat but with the number 54.

● Ask the children to use their lists to find the highest common factor of 36 and 54. Remind them what the term *highest common factor* means. Repeat with the pair of numbers 60 and 48.

● Invite the children to note any similarities and differences between the number of factors in each of the four numbers used so far. The numbers 48, 54 and 60 each have an even number of factors. The number 36 has an odd number of factors. Invite them to explain why this is so.

Activity development

● Demonstrate how to form a factor tree for the number 48. Complete the tree and set out 48 as the product of its prime factors, that is, $48 = 2 \times 2 \times 2 \times 2 \times 3$. Explain that factor trees provide important insights into the properties of numbers. Ask them to create a factor tree for 60 and compare it with the one for 48. Use their observations as the basis for discussion, but encourage them to look not only at the individual factors produced, but also at the number of factors.

● Return to the number 60. Ask them to create the factor tree by forming the first two branches in a different way. That is, they can partition 60 as 5×12 or 10×6 or 15×4 or 20×3. However, they must choose a different starting point to that used in the first attempt.

● Ask, for each of the different ways to partition 60: *What do you notice about the final list of factors?* They should conclude that all of the trees produce the same final list, namely $2 \times 2 \times 3 \times 5$.

● Introduce the children to photocopiable page 49. Make sure they are happy to find factor trees on their own.

Review

● Check that the children have formed the trees correctly. ($24 = 2 \times 2 \times 2 \times 3$; $56 = 2 \times 2 \times 2 \times 7$; $100 = 2 \times 2 \times 5 \times 5$; $81 = 3 \times 3 \times 3 \times 3$. The final part asks them for the factor tree for 210. The importance of this number is that it is the product of the first four prime numbers, $210 = 2 \times 3 \times 5 \times 7$. Each of the others had a repeated factor.

● Ask: *What would be special about factor trees with no branches?* They should recognise that such a tree starts with a prime number.

> **Next steps**
> ● Invite the children to form factor trees for larger numbers. They could also try to see how to use factor trees to find the highest common factor of a number.

Factor trees

■ Here is a factor tree for the number 42.

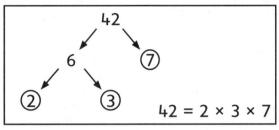

$$42 = 2 \times 3 \times 7$$

To make it we need two numbers which multiply to make 42. We have chosen 6 × 7.

■ If a number in the tree is prime put a ring around it.

■ If it is not prime, continue by finding two more numbers that you can multiply to make that number. Continue until all numbers are prime.

The number at the top is the product of all the prime numbers with rings around them.

1. Make factor trees for 24, 56, 100 and 81. Write each number as the product of its prime factors. The factor tree for 24 has been started for you.

24 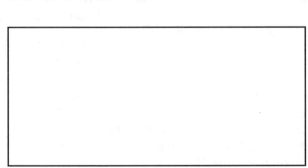	56
100	81

2. Form a factor tree for the number 210 and say what is special about the numbers in the tree.

Cuboid numbers

Learning objectives
(Y5) Use/apply strand:
Explore patterns, properties and relationships and propose a general statement involving numbers.
(Y5) Knowledge strand:
Identify pairs of factors of two-digit whole numbers and find common multiples.
(Y6) Knowledge strand:
Recognise that prime numbers have only two factors and identify prime numbers less than 100; find the prime factors of two-digit whole numbers.

Expected prior knowledge
● Understand factors and multiples of numbers, within the normal range of the multiplication tables.

You will need
Photocopiable page 51 (one per child); a large number of linking cubes.

Key vocabulary
cuboid, cube number, square number, factor, multiple, prime number, composite number

Activity introduction
● Present the numbers 1, 4, 9, 16 and 25. Ask the children: *What are these numbers?* (If necessary, carry on with the square numbers, 36, 49 and so on.) Once they have recognised these, ask why they are called square numbers. Some children may not associate these numbers with the area of a square. For example, 25cm² is the area of a square with sides of 5cm.
● Introduce the children to rectangle numbers and discuss their properties: These are numbers that represent the area of a rectangle or the size of an array. For example, 12 is a rectangle number because it is the area of a 4 × 3 rectangle. Alternatively, 12 can be made from four rows of 3. Rectangles have to have more than one row or column. Otherwise all numbers are rectangle numbers and the definition is unhelpful. For example, 7 is not a rectangle number because its only rectangle is 1 × 7, or one row of 7. This distinction allows us to identify prime numbers as those that can only make rectangles with one row.
● Invite the children to discuss why some numbers, such as 24, can be formed into several different rectangles. Ask: *How can we identify those rectangle numbers that can be made in several different ways?*

Activity development
● Show the children a 2 × 2 × 2 cube composed of eight smaller cubes. Ask: *How many cubes are there in the model?* Explain that this means that 8 is a cube number. Ask: *Can you find the next two or three cube numbers?* (27, 64 and 125.)
● Display a model made from 12 cubes. Once they have recognised the shape of the solid and the number of cubes it contains, suggest that this means that 12 is a cuboid number. Explain the rule that all cuboids have to have at least two cubes along each side.
● Ask for another cuboid number. Invite them to construct it to check.
● Ask the children to construct a cuboid for the cuboid number 40. If each child has made the same one, keep a copy for reference and challenge them for another way to make it. (The two cuboids are 2 × 2 × 10 and 2 × 4 × 5.)
● Give out copies of photocopiable page 51 and explain how they should record any cuboids found.
● Towards the end of the main activity, invite them to make some of their solutions from small cubes to illustrate their answers.

Review
● Review the cuboids found. The smallest cuboid with two distinct solids is 24, made either as 2 × 2 × 6 or 2 × 3 × 4. There are several numbers with many cuboids, but 72, 84 and 96 are good examples.

Next steps
● Explain that the cuboid numbers above, which make lots of distinct cuboids, are all multiples of 12. Ask why this is.
● Invite them to investigate the cuboids of numbers that are powers of 2, such as 32, 64 or 128. One key observation is that these can all be cut in half to make alternative cuboids.

Cuboid numbers

◼ Cuboids can be made by joining small cubes together. The number of cubes needed is called a cuboid number.
Here is a picture of the cuboid number 12.

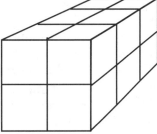

1. How can you make a cuboid from 30 cubes? Write its dimensions here.

2. Find two different cuboids for the cuboid number 60.

3. Find three different cuboids for the cuboid number 100.

4. What is the smallest cuboid number that has two different-shaped cuboids? Describe the sizes of the two cuboids and explain why it is the smallest.

5. Find the number below 100 which has the most cuboids. Each one must be distinct. Use the back of this page to make a list of them all.

Divisibility tests

Activity introduction

● As a mental starter, ask the children for a multiple of 2, and another. Ask: *What is the largest two-digit multiple of 2? Can you give me a three-digit multiple of 2 where the digits add to 10?*

● Continue with questions about multiples of 3. *What is the largest two-digit multiple of 3? What is the smallest three-digit multiple of 3?* Once they decide the latter is 102, ask how they got this answer. Invite them to write down several multiples of 3 and add the digits. What do they notice? They may already know the rule that the digit sum of a multiple of 3 is also a multiple of 3.

● If this idea is new, allow time to explore this property for different numbers, multiples of 4 and 5 for example, or all numbers from 2 to 9.

● Ensure that the children realise that it is only multiples of 3 and 9 for which the digit sum of a number is also a multiple of 3 or 9.

Activity development

● The main activity extends the rules for divisibility tests to the numbers 4, 6 and 8. Ask the children to consider the number 52. Ask: *How do you know it is a multiple of 4?* One way is to consider 52 = 48 + 4 or 52 = 40 + 12. Explain why both ideas are useful. You could also note that 52 = 60 - 8. In all cases, the number 52 has been partitioned into two numbers, both multiples of 4.

● Ask the children to write a column of four or five numbers, each of which is a multiple of 4. Ask them to halve each of their first set of numbers and write it alongside. What do they notice about this second column? (Numbers are all even.) Explain that they can test for multiples of 4 by halving a number and checking that the answer is even.

● Ask them to write down the first few multiples of 6, allowing time to discuss any properties. Refine definitions if necessary so that they recognise that multiples of 6 are multiples of 2 and 3 or even multiples of 9. Ask them to work through photocopiable page 53 individually.

Review

● Go through the first part of the activity, but focus on refining a rule for multiples of 8. Guide them towards checking to see if a number is even after halving and halving again.

● Invite the children to offer the smallest number that is divisible by 2, 3, 4, 5, 6, 8 and 9, and to provide a checking method. If you need to go through it in detail, begin with 72 (8 × 9). 72 will also be divisible by 2, 3 and 4, because these numbers are factors of 8 and 9. It is divisible by 6, because 72 is an even multiple of 3. So they only need to find a multiple of 72 that is also a multiple of 5. The 72-times table yields 360 = 5 × 72 as the smallest number. (The mathematics of this method is not strictly rigorous, but is sufficient at this stage.)

Next steps

● Invite the children to find the largest three-digit (or four-digit) number that is divisible by 2, 3, 4, 5, 6, 8, 9.

● Very able learners could use the internet to research divisibility tests for the number 7. Most will find this too demanding.

Learning objectives
(Y5) Knowledge strand:
Recall quickly multiplication facts up to 10 × 10 and use them to multiply pairs of multiples of 10 and 100; derive quickly corresponding division facts.
(Y5) Knowledge strand:
Identify pairs of factors of two-digit whole numbers and find common multiples.

Expected prior knowledge
● Understand multiples and their properties for even numbers, and multiples of 5 and 10.

You will need
Photocopiable page 53 (one per child); a set of 0-9 number cards for each child.

Key vocabulary
multiple, factor, divisibility

Brainteaser link
16. Think of a number

Divisibility tests

◼ Multiples of 2 are even.
Multiples of 3 have a digit sum that is also a multiple of 3.
Multiples of 4 can be halved to give an even number.
Multiples of 5 end in 0 or 5.
Multiples of 6 are even multiples of 3.
Multiples of 9 have a digit sum that is also a multiple of 9.

1. Use the above rules to check the following numbers. The first has been done for you.

144 is a multiple of 2, 3, 4 and 6.

225 is a multiple of _____

390 is a multiple of _____

960 is a multiple of _____

2. Multiples of 4 can be halved to give an even number. Extend this idea and invent a rule to test for multiples of 8. Show your method works with some examples.

3. Find the smallest number which is a multiple of all of 2, 3, 4, 5, 6, 8 and 9.

Sieving for primes

Activity introduction

● Discuss a suitable way to define a prime number. Some children may offer: *a prime number is one which is divisible by one and itself.* Ask for some examples. (Check that children can spell the word *divisible* correctly.)

● Ask the children how the number 1 fits into this definition - is it prime? Give them some time to think. Some children may argue that one is a prime number, others that it is not. The definition is ambiguous.

● Offer the following more robust and useful definition: *a prime number has precisely two factors.* Ask them again how the number 1 fits into this definition. It is clear that 1 is not a prime number as it has only one factor.

Activity development

● Ask: *How can we tell quickly that 475 is not a prime number?* Continue with less obvious examples such as 321, or 909.

● Ask the children to discuss how they could test a more difficult example, such as 437. This will appear to be prime on first examination. However, it is the product of 19 and 23.

● Once the children are aware that 437 = 19 × 23, ask them how we can tell there are no other factors. (It is because both 19 and 23 are prime numbers.)

● Go through photocopiable page 55 and explain how the 'sieve' works. Encourage the children to shade the squares lightly.

Review

● Write the list of primes less than 100 for the children to confirm that they are correct. (2, 3, 5, 7, 11, 13, 17, 19, 23, 29, 31, 37, 41, 43, 47, 53, 59, 61, 67, 71, 73, 79, 83, 89, 97.)

● Ask the children to explain why we do not need to shade multiples of numbers above 7. They may offer the closed response that after you have shaded multiples of 7 you have them all. Ask them what is special about 7. Remind them that factors of numbers are usually found in pairs. That is, once you know that 3 is a factor of 24, you know that 8 is also a factor of 24 because 3 × 8 = 24. By extending this line of enquiry, argue that we only have to test factors up to the square root of the largest number in the list. We do not need to test 10, 9 or 8 because they were crossed out when smaller multiples were tested. Once we have eliminated multiples of 7 we have eliminated 7 × 13 = 91, and hence a multiple of 13.

Learning objectives
(Y5) Knowledge strand: Identify pairs of factors of two-digit whole numbers and find common multiples, eg for 6 and 9.
(Y6) Knowledge strand: Recognise that prime numbers have only two factors and identify prime numbers less than 100.

Expected prior knowledge
● Understand the use of factors and multiples of a number.

You will need
Photocopiable page 55; a number of different-coloured pencils for each group (coloured pencils rather than felt tips); calculators for part of the 'Activity development'.

Key vocabulary
prime, prime factors, multiple, highest common factor, divisible, divisibility test, sieve

Next steps
● The children could extend the 'sieve' by using a larger grid. The most able could produce a sieve of any size using a spreadsheet. Another avenue of enquiry is to research the Greek mathematician Eratosthenes, who first devised the sieve method and gave it his name. There are online sieves that the children may find interesting.

Name _____

Sieving for primes

◗ Follow these rules to 'sieve' for the prime numbers up to 100.

1. Shade the number 1, as it is not a prime number.

2. Now choose a new colour for shading.

3. Find the first unshaded square.

4. Leave it unshaded, but shade all of its multiples lightly.

5. Return to rule 2 and repeat the process.

1	2	3	4	5	6	7	8	9	10
11	12	13	14	15	16	17	18	19	20
21	22	23	24	25	26	27	28	29	30
31	32	33	34	35	36	37	38	39	40
41	42	43	44	45	46	47	48	49	50
51	52	53	54	55	56	57	58	59	60
61	62	63	64	65	66	67	68	69	70
71	72	73	74	75	76	77	78	79	80
81	82	83	84	85	86	87	88	89	90
91	92	93	94	95	96	97	98	99	100

◗ List the unshaded numbers here. These are all the prime numbers less than 100.

_____

_____

_____

◗ Explain why you did not need to shade any multiples higher than 7.

_____

_____

_____

The square root of 12

Activity introduction

- Remind the children what a square number is. Ask them for 6 squared, 9 squared and so on. Continue with other numbers until they are secure with all square numbers to $144 = 12^2$.
- Introduce them to the notation for squaring numbers. Explain that we need a shorthand form. Write the following sentence to show that mathematical expressions can be very succinct: Seven squared = seven times seven = $7 \times 7 = 7^2$. Emphasise the correct use of the equals sign in this sentence.
- Ask the children to draw up a table of three columns; one column for the numbers 1-6, one for their square and an empty column. Explain that the empty column should contain the difference between adjacent square numbers.
- Once they have completed the table for five numbers, invite them to comment on the

Number	Square	Diff
1	1	1
2	4	3
3	9	5
4	16	7
5	25	9
6	36	11

pattern in the difference column. Ask them to use this pattern to produce the next square number. This is shown in the shaded row of the table opposite. That is; $25 + 11 = 36$ must be 6^2.

Activity development

- Explain the concept of *square root*. If we are given a square number such as 16, we can ask: *What number multiplied by itself gives 16?* Test their understanding by asking for the square roots of 36, 64, 121, and so on. Use any that were discussed as square numbers in the introduction.
- Set the square root in a practical context. Say: *I have a square garden with an area of 81 square metres, what is the length of a side of my garden?* Continue with: *I have another square vegetable plot in my garden, with an area of 12 square metres. What is the length of one side of the plot?* Give them time to realise that the answer is between 3 and 4 metres and that it is not 3.5 metres.
- Introduce photocopiable page 57. Explain the there are two methods for finding the answer. The first is to refine guesses based on the difference between the squares of numbers and the area, 12. The second method invites them to be more systematic. They must find two numbers whose squares are either side of 12. A new number is formed, the average of these two. This process continues until the children are happy with their answer.

Review

- Some children may have become determined to work out the answer to a greater degree of accuracy than required. They could be invited to share their results.

Next steps

- Very able learners could be introduced to a more advanced method for finding the square root of 12. Take any approximate value, such as 3.5. Find $^{12}/_{3.5} = 4.43$ (to two decimal places). If one number is too small, the other will be too big. Find a new number from the average of these two. This process is continued. It converges to the square root of 12 quickly.

Learning objectives
(Y6) Use/apply strand: Solve multi-step problems involving decimals; choose and use appropriate (and efficient) strategies at each stage, including calculator use.
(Y6) Knowledge strand: Use approximations, inverse operations and tests of divisibility to check results.
(Y6) Calculate strand: Use a calculator to solve problems involving multi-step calculations.
(Y6/Y7) Knowledge strand: Make and justify estimates and approximations to calculations.

Expected prior knowledge
- Understand square numbers.

You will need
Photocopiable page 57; a calculator, preferably one without a square root key (one per child).

Key vocabulary
square number, square root, approximation, estimation, trial and improvement, inverse

Brainteaser link
6. 1001 calculations

The square root of 12

◼ I have a vegetable plot with an area of 12 square metres.
How long is the side of the plot?

Method 1

◼ We know that $3^2 = 3 \times 3 = 9$ and $4^2 = 4 \times 4 = 16$, so we are looking for a number between 3 and 4. Use trial and improvement to get the square root of 12 correct to two decimal places.

Number	Square	Difference	Too small or too big?
3	9	3	Too small
4	16	4	Too big
3.5			

Method 2

◼ Find two numbers near to the square root of 12. One number must be too small and one number must be too big. Make a new number from the average of these two.

Number	Square	Difference	Too small or too big?
3	9	3	Too small
4	16	4	Too big
3.5			

If you need more space for your workings out, use the back of this page.

Decimal division

Activity introduction

● Ask the children to give you two different whole numbers whose product is 100. Explore all of the possible answers, such as 1 and 100, 2 and 50, 4 and 25, and 5 and 20.

● Ask the children why there is no pairing with the number 3. Discuss with them the fact that 3 is not a factor of 100.

● Ask for some more pairs of numbers whose product is 100, if we allow any numbers (i.e. including decimals) to be used. Give them time to think and to discuss their ideas with each other. If you need to offer more support, suggest that they could begin with one of the earlier products, such as 5 and 20, and alter it. Useful products which can easily be formed using this method include 2.5 and 40, and 8 and 12.5.

● Conclude by drawing children's attention to the relationship between the pairs of numbers 4 and 25, and 8 and 12.5. Notice that one of the pair has been doubled and the other has been halved. The product remains the same.

Activity development

● Provide each child with photocopiable page 59 and hand out the spinners or dice needed to generate numbers. Since the challenge on the activity page has several rules, it may be worth going through them with the class to ensure that every child understands what they have to do.

● Go through the first example and ask all of the children to give a good estimate of $100 \div 3.7$. Review the estimates offered by the group and then discuss strategies for getting close. For example, we know that $100 \div 4$ is 25, so $100 \div 3.7$ must be a little over 25. (The nearest whole number is 27.)

● The children should now be ready to play the game.

Review

● Invite some children to feed back to the whole class any strategies they used and found successful. Use these strategies as the basis of a discussion.

● In particular, focus on efficient ways to use known number facts to help with a difficult estimate or calculation. For example, we can deduce that a number between 4 and 5 will go into 100 between 20 and 25 times, since $100 \div 4 = 25$ and $100 \div 5 = 20$.

> **Next steps**
> ● Discuss the relationship between pairs of numbers whose product is 100 and percentages. For example, if $4 \times 25 = 100$ then $4 \times 25\% = 100\% = 1$ and so $25\% = 1/4$.

Learning objectives

(Y5) Use/apply strand:
Solve one- and two-step problems involving whole numbers and decimals and all four operations, choosing and using appropriate methods, including calculator use.

(Y6) Calculate strand:
Calculate mentally with integers and decimals, eg U.t + U.t, TU × U, HTU ÷ U, U.t × U, U.t ÷ U.

(Y6/Y7) Calculate strand:
Consolidate and extend mental methods of calculation to include decimals.

Expected prior knowledge

● Estimate multiplications and divisions involving one- and two-digit numbers.

You will need

Photocopiable page 59 (one per child); 0–9 spinners or dice (two per pair/group); calculators.

Key vocabulary

decimal, division, difference, product

Decimal division

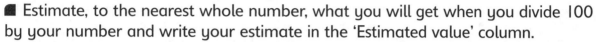

■ This is a game or challenge for any number of players.
Each player needs a copy of this activity sheet.
You also need two 0–9 spinners or dice between you.
■ Use the spinners or dice to produce a decimal number
between 0 and 9.9 and write it in the first column of the table.
The first number has been done for you.
■ Estimate, to the nearest whole number, what you will get when you divide 100
by your number and write your estimate in the 'Estimated value' column.
■ Calculate the value, correct to the nearest whole number, and write it in the
'Calculated value' column.
■ Find the difference between your estimate and the calculated value and write
it in the 'Difference column'.
■ Decide who is the closest and put a tick or a cross in the 'Closest' column.
The winner is the player with the most ticks in your group.

Number produced	Estimated value	Calculated value	Difference	Closest?
3.7				

Grid tricks

Learning objectives
(Y5) Calculate strand:
Refine and use efficient
methods to multiply
HTU × U, TU × TU and
U.t × U.

**Expected prior
knowledge**
● Use the grid method for
multiplication of TU × TU.
● Mentally calculate U × TU
with confidence.

You will need
OHP or whiteboard;
photocopiable page 61 (one
per child).

Key vocabulary
distributive law (introduce
as appropriate)

Brainteaser link
13. Diagonal sums

Activity introduction
● Write the calculation 8 × 23 in horizontal format on an OHP or
interactive whiteboard. Ask the children to discuss the different ways of
doing the calculation. Possible methods include partitioning into 8 × 20
+ 8 × 3 = 184 or noticing that 8 × 25 = 200, so 8 × 23 = 8 × 25 - 8 × 2
= 200 - 16 = 184. Some children may partition into 10 × 23 - 2 × 23 =
230 - 46 = 184, but this is a little clumsy.
● Set out the calculation in the standard grid method format. Show that
this arrangement is similar to one of the mental partitioning methods.
● Continue with the calculation 19 × 28, again setting it out in grid
format as shown below left. Set out the table but leave the entries
blank. Invite the children to fill them in. Now set out the calculation with
the numbers partitioned as shown below right. While this may not seem
natural (or sensible), it mirrors
an efficient mental method of
partitioning: 19 × 28 = 20 × 28
- 1 × 28 = 20 × 20 + 20 × 8 - 1
× 28 = 560 - 28 = 532.

×	20	8	
10	200	80	280
9	180	72	252
		Total	532

×	20	8	
20	400	160	560
-1	-20	-8	-28
		Total	532

Activity development
● Introduce photocopiable page 61. Explain that the children are going
to work in pairs to explore other ways of setting out grid calculations.
● Draw their attention to the processes and steps involved in the
calculation and invite them to recognise links between efficient written
methods such as this and efficient mental methods. For example, an
efficient way to calculate 19 × 8 mentally is to reform the calculation as
20 × 8 - 1 × 8 = 160 - 8 = 152.

Review
● Check the calculations from the main part of the activity. Invite
commentary on the final question of 34 × 999 and work through the
method of 34 × 1000 - 34 × 1 = 33966.
● This extension of the grid method is important because it is the
method underlying the expansion of brackets in algebra and will help to
give the children confidence with the distributive law.
● Explain this to the children and, if there is time, return to the
calculation of 19 × 28 (from the introduction), setting it out as shown
on the right.
● A key objective as children make progress is to
help them recognise links between different parts of
mathematics. Your own insight may be strengthened
by multiplying out the product (3x - 2)(2x -1) and
comparing your solution with the grid.

×	30	-2	
20	600	-40	560
-1	-30	2	-28
		Total	532

Next steps
● If children have adopted other standard written methods, invite them
to make comparisons between the mathematics needed to perform a
multiplication when using these other methods and when using the grid
method. They should focus on similarities and differences between
methods, rather than their preference for one method.

Name _____

Grid tricks

◼ The first grid below shows the steps in the grid method for multiplying 8 by 19, to give 152.

This method produces the same calculations as an efficient mental method for multiplying 8 by 19: for example, 8 × 19 = (8 × 10) + (8 × 9).

◼ Complete the other two grids, which show the same calculation. In each of them the numbers to be multiplied have been partitioned differently, but the result is the same.

×	10	9	
8	80	72	152
		Total	152

×	20	-1	
8			
		Total	152

×	19		
10			
-2			
		Total	152

◼ Try to convert each of the methods above into an efficient mental method.

◼ The first grid below shows the steps in the grid method for multiplying 23 by 19, to give 437.

◼ Complete the other two grids, which show the same calculation. In each of them the numbers to be multiplied have been partitioned differently, but the result is the same.

×	10	9	
20	200	180	380
3	30	27	57
		Total	437

×	20	-1	
20			
3			
		Total	437

×	20	-1	
30			
-7			
		Total	437

◼ Try to convert each of the methods above into an efficient mental method.

◼ Set out the calculation 28 × 31 in three different ways, using the grids below.

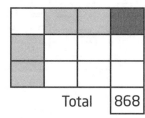

Total 868

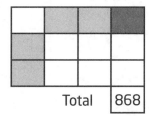

Total 868

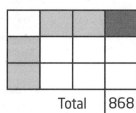

Total 868

◼ Try to convert each of the methods above into an efficient mental method.

◼ Use the grid method to multiply 34 by 999 in two different ways. Set the calculation out in a grid of your own on the back of this page.

Sweet stuff

Activity introduction

- Tell the children that the cubes are worth a lot of money and each colour has a different price. Put a red and a yellow cube together, with a combined price tag of £5. Ask them for possible prices for each cube.
- Now put out a red and a blue cube, with a combined price tag of £6. Leave the original cubes out for comparison. Invite further suggestions as to the prices.
- Finally put out one cube of each colour and a combined price tag of £9, alongside the others. Allow the children some time to discuss the problem before inviting comments.
- If they are struggling, suggest that they consider the price of the first two groups together. Children should realise that these together have two red cubes, one yellow one and one blue one. This is the same as the final pile but with an additional red cube, thus allowing them to deduce the price of a red cube is £2, a yellow cube is £3 and a blue cube is £4.

Activity development

- Provide each child with photocopiable page 63. The sheet presents the children with six different gift boxes of sweets. Each has a different composition of sweets and some have a cuddly toy included. The task is to work out the price of each item.
- The children may find the raised level of complexity daunting. If so, suggest that they focus on the two boxes at the bottom of the sheet first. This will help them to calculate the price of a Chocobrick.
- If children finish the task, ask them to make up a new gift box using the prices they have found. You can use this to check if they have the correct values without revealing the prices to others still working on the problem.

Solution

Chocobrick 40p, Nutto 50p, Munchymint 60p, Teddy £1.50, Box 30p.

Review

- A key issue with this activity is the method of solution. It is designed to raise the level of reasoning used. Therefore, it is important that much of the review is given over to discussing alternative methods of solution. One approach is to use a table (right).

	Chocobrick 40p	Nutto 50p	Munchymint 60p	Teddy 150p	Box 30p	Total cost (pence)
A	1	1		1	1	270
B	1	1	1		1	180
C	1		1	1	1	280
D	3				1	150
E	1	1	1	1	1	330
F		1	1	1	1	290

Next steps

- The children can make up similar problems for others to solve. This is difficult as they need to make sure the problem is possible but not too easy. Set a context where they can explore the variables. For example, a café menu may include sausage, egg, beans, mushrooms and chips. Customers choose meals made up from a combination of these, but the café works out the price by adding up the prices of individual items.

Learning objectives
(Y6) Use/apply strand:
Explain reasoning and conclusions, using symbols as appropriate.

Expected prior knowledge
- Solve multi-stage problems which do not offer many clues as to the required method of solution.

You will need
Plastic cubes (three each of red, yellow and blue); photocopiable page 63 (one per child); paper for jottings; calculators; removable stickers (for price tags).

Key vocabulary
deduce, reasoning

Brainteaser link
11. Last one loses

Sweet stuff

◀ The Sweet Stuff company make gift boxes with sweets. Sometimes the boxes include a small cuddly teddy. The price of a gift box is calculated by adding together the price of the various items and then adding on the price of the box itself.

◀ The sweets in each box are selected from Chocobrick, Nutto, and Munchymint. The price list for each item has been lost.

◀ Use the prices on the gift boxes to work out the cost of each item.

A — £2·70

B — £1·80

C — £2·80

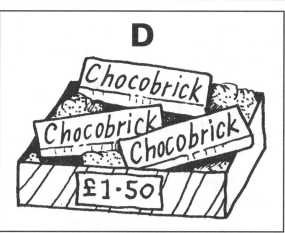

D — £1·50

E — £3·30

F — £2·90

Broken calculator

Activity introduction

- Revisit the grid method of multiplication. Set out a simple grid for multiplying 8 by 23 (see right).
- Ask the children how the grid method uses the distributive law. If this activity is being used as an introduction to the

×	20	3	
8	160	24	184
Total			184

distributive law, ask them how the grid method supports an efficient mental method of calculating 8 × 23. Use of the distributive law leads to 8 × 23 = 8 × 20 + 8 × 3. More formally, this may be written as 8 × (20 + 3) = 8 × 20 + 8 × 3, which shows the distributive law clearly.
- Ask the children to reproduce 7 × 42 in the same way.
- Continue with 12 × 15, which can be tackled in more than one way. For example:

  12 × 15 = 10 × 15 + 2 × 15 = 150 + 30 = 180
  12 × 15 = 12 × 10 + 12 × 5 = 120 + 60 = 180

- Finally, ask the children to represent 38 × 6 using the distributive law. The most sensible way is 38 × 6 = 40 × 6 - 2 × 6 = 240 - 12 = 228, but it is worth discussing the merits of different ways.

Activity development

- Hand out copies of photocopiable page 65 and a calculator to each child or pair. The activity requires a secure understanding of the distributive law and invites children to use this to solve a problem. They imagine that only the even numbers on their calculator work and devise ways of using the distributive law to represent a calculation.
- The use of brackets is intended to help them understand the use of the distributive law. Brackets also make sure that the type of calculator being used does not impose its own calculating rules. Return to the calculation above. Use a scientific calculator and type in 40 × 6 - 2 × 6 =. The answer is 228. However, with a simple, four-function calculator, the answer is 1428.
- The final part of the activity invites the children to find the area of a rectangle with their broken calculator. The calculations are similar to those already carried out but the intention here is for the children to apply what they have learned in a new context.

Review

- Compare the different approaches children take and make sure that they are mathematically sound.
- Compare the variety of ways of illustrating the final example. Invite children to comment on the similarities between the method of dividing up the rectangle and the use of brackets in the previous calculations.

Learning objectives

(Y6/Y7) Use/apply strand:
Solve problems by breaking down complex calculations into simpler steps; choose and use operations and calculation strategies appropriate to the numbers and context; try alternative approaches to overcome difficulties; present, interpret and compare solutions.
(Y6/Y7) Calculate strand:
Understand how the commutative and distributive laws, and the relationships between operations can be used to calculate more efficiently; use the order of operations, including brackets.

Expected prior knowledge

- Understand the distributive law for multiplication and recognise how to reorganise a calculation and to present it in an alternative way.

You will need

Photocopiable page 65 (one per child/pair); calculators (not broken); set of 0-9 digit cards.

Key vocabulary

distributive law

Next steps

- Invite the children to analyse the use of the distributive law evident within the grid method of calculating 37 × 23.
- Invite the children to investigate the differences between the answers given by a scientific calculator and a simple 'four-function' calculator. This idea will be developed further in Lesson 20 'Can you trust your calculator?'.

Name _____

Broken calculator

■ On your calculator only the even digits work. You must devise ways to get the exact answer to the calculations below, without using any odd digits. You must also try to use as few key presses as possible.

■ In the 'Setting out' box, write the calculation you used, including brackets, where needed. Count the key presses and write the number in the last box.

Calculation	Setting out	Answer	Number of keys pressed
38 × 8			
43 × 6			
64 × 11			
68 × 18			
92 × 4			
37 × 5			
246 × 135			
135 × 357			
361 × 250			

■ Show how to find the area of the rectangle below using your broken calculator.
■ Divide the rectangle into smaller shapes to illustrate your solution.

164m

256m

Can you trust your calculator?

Learning objectives
(Y6) Use/apply strand: Solve multi-step problems; choose and use appropriate calculation strategies at each stage, including calculator use.
(Y6) Calculate strand: Use a calculator to solve problems involving multi-step calculations.
(Y6/Y7) Calculate strand: Understand how the distributive law can be used to calculate more efficiently; use the order of operations, including brackets.

Expected prior knowledge
● Display some knowledge of the distributive law.
● Use both a four-function (simple) calculator and a scientific calculator.

You will need
Two calculators per pair (one must be a simple, four-function calculator with brackets, the other must be a simple, standard scientific calculator); photocopiable page 67.

Key vocabulary
distributive law, brackets

Brainteaser link
5. Target numbers

Activity introduction
● Give each pair a simple four-function calculator and a scientific calculator. Some children may not be familiar with a scientific calculator, so give them time to explore the differences. Suggest that they do not press too many 'unknown' buttons on the scientific calculator at this stage or they may become 'lost'.
● Ask the children to perform the calculation 2 + 3 × 4 mentally. All of them should give the answer of 20. Ask them to confirm this using the simple calculator. Now ask them to confirm it using the scientific calculator. The result that 2 + 3 × 4 = 14 will surprise many. Give them a chance to check and appreciate that the calculators give different answers to the question.
● Ask them to try 3 × 4 + 5 on both calculators. (The answer is 17 on both.) Ask them to try 3 + 4 × 5 on both and discuss what they have found so far. Ask why these 'similar' examples produce different results.
● Explain that the simple calculator performs its operations in the order you type them, whereas the scientific calculator looks at the whole calculation and does multiplication and division before addition and subtraction.
● Ask the children to find two calculations that produce the same answer on both calculators and two that produce different answers.

Activity development
● Explain that we can use brackets to make the answers the same on both calculators. The brackets force the calculator to do the calculation in the order we want it to. Remind the children of the distributive law, in which brackets perform an important function.
● Return to some of the examples from the introduction. Ask them to calculate (3 + 4) × 5 on both calculators and discuss the result. Repeat with the calculation 3 + (4 × 5).
● Ask the children to put brackets into 2 + 3 × 4 + 5 to make the answer 29 on both calculators. Give them a little time to explore this problem, before going over it.
● Give each child a copy of photocopiable page 67. Encourage them to look for rules and patterns in the examples and to work the calculations out mentally where possible.

Review
● Explore some of the answers where necessary, concentrating on rules and making sure that all children understand the role being played by brackets and essential differences between the calculators. The brackets needed in the final activity are used to simplify the calculation to 5 × 5 × 4. The solution is: (4 + 1) × (8 + 3 - 6) × (3 × 3 - 2).

Next steps
● Invite the children to explore nested brackets. Give them the calculation 3 + (5 × (7 - 3)) and ask them what the answer is. The answer of 23 arises because of the nesting of the brackets; the inner one is performed first. Ask them to put brackets into 2 + 3 × 4 + 5 - 6 to give the answer 23 on both calculators. The calculation is 2 + (3 × (4 + 5)) - 6.

Can you trust your calculator?

1. For each calculation:
◗ Write the answer you get with a simple calculator.
◗ Write the answer you get with a scientific calculator.
◗ Use brackets so that the answer you get with your simple calculator is the same as the one you get with your scientific calculator.

Without brackets	Simple calculator	Scientific calculator	With brackets
3 + 5 × 2 + 7			3 + (5 × 2) + 7
3 × 3 + 4 × 6			
5 + 5 × 5 – 5			
60 – 8 × 5			
16 -12 ÷ 4 + 3			
3 + 7 × 5 + 3 – 2			
7 × 7 – 7 × 7 + 7			
1 + 2 × 3 – 4 + 5 × 6			
2 × 2 + 2 × 2 – 2 ÷ 2			

2. Insert two sets of brackets in each of these calculations to make the all the answers 72, with both calculators.

4 + 5 × 7 + 1
3 × 5 + 3 × 5 – 3
4 + 2 × 3 × 2 + 2
3 × 3 + 3 × 3 + 1
6 × 4 + 2 × 4 – 2

3. Insert as many brackets as you need to make this calculation total 100 with both calculators.

4 + 1 × 8 + 3 – 6 × 3 × 2 – 2

Chocolate fudge cake

Activity introduction

● Create price labels for three different boxes of cornflakes. These are 500g for £1.20, 750g for £1.60, 1kg for £2.00. If possible, have a box of each available and label them.

● Explain the term, 'value for money'. Ask: *Which of the boxes is the best value for money?* Give them time to discuss the problem.

● Tell the children that you normally buy the small box (500g) and that you get eight portions from it. Ask them to work out the cost of a portion. Continue by asking them to calculate mentally how many portions you would get from each of the other boxes. (12 and 16 respectively.)

● Using the calculator ask them to work out the cost per portion of the other boxes. Ask: *Why are the larger boxes cheaper per portion?*

Activity development

● Tell them that you have used up 200g from your 500g box of cornflakes. Ask them to calculate the value of the cornflakes left. Allow them to discuss different ways to do this in pairs give them time to agree an answer. (72p)

● Discuss the various ways of tackling the problem and make sure the children are comfortable with calculating the fraction of a quantity. Make sure they are aware of the connections between fractions and their decimal equivalents. For example the 200g eaten from a 500g box could be represented in the three different ways: $^2/_5$, 0.4 and 40%.

● Introduce photocopiable page 69 and explain the nature of the task. Encourage the children to work in pairs and invite them to check their calculations by trying different ways to solve each problem. Finally explain to the children that some of the prices will need rounding and that they should do this to an appropriate degree of accuracy. Leave them to decide what this is.

Review

● Invite the children to explain how they worked out the cost of each item. Some items, such as the eggs, should be calculated mentally and precisely. Other items, such as the sugar, lead to fractions of a penny and will require a calculator. Make sure the children have rounded these prices appropriately.

Learning objectives
(Y5) Use/apply strand: Solve one- and two-step problems involving whole numbers and decimals and all four operations, choosing and using appropriate calculation strategies, including calculator use.
(Y5) Calculate strand: Find fractions using division and percentages of numbers and quantities.
(Y5) Calculate strand: Use a calculator to solve problems, including those involving decimals or fractions; interpret the display correctly in the context of measurement.

Expected prior knowledge
● Understand how to convert between fractions and decimals with a calculator.

You will need
Photocopiable page 69 (one per pair); calculators for each child.

Key vocabulary
fraction, percentage, proportion (It may also be worth checking that children are aware of the names of the main ingredients used in the cake.)

Next steps
● Invite the children to set up the table on a spreadsheet and to use the calculation or formula features of the spreadsheet to do the calculation.
● Tell the children that the cake is intended for eight people. Ask them to use the spreadsheet to work out the ingredients and cost of a cake for 12 people.

Name _____

Chocolate fudge cake

■ Work out the cost of the chocolate fudge cake by completing the table showing the prices of the main ingredients used.

Ingredients

For the cake	For the filling and topping
175g self-raising flour	125g brown sugar
175g butter	125g dark chocolate pieces
175g brown sugar	50g butter
3 eggs	200g evaporated milk
25g cocoa powder	

Item	Package size	Package cost	Quantity needed	Cost

How big is a million?

Learning objectives
(Y6) Use/apply strand:
Solve multi-step problems, and problems involving fractions, decimals and percentages; choose and use appropriate calculation strategies at each stage, including calculator use.
(Y6) Calculate strand: Use a calculator to solve problems involving multi-step calculations.

Expected prior knowledge
● Comfortable with large numbers, such as 1 000 000. Efficient use of a calculator is essential.

You will need
Calculators (one per child); access to data sources, particularly the internet are needed, if the children are to research the information needed; 1kg rice; photocopiable page 71 (one per child).

Key vocabulary
one million, one hundred thousand

Activity introduction

● Children need to become accustomed to working with large numbers. Start with a number such as 27. Ask the children to successively multiply it by 10. Insist that they speak the result correctly, in words. Make sure that all children are confident with all of the numbers up to 2 700 000. Try the activity in reverse. Ask them to successively divide 34 000 000, until they reach 34, speaking each number correctly.

● Ask them how long it would take to count to 1 000 000 if they had to say every number correctly. Allow several minutes to discuss this and to come up with questions and ideas. There needs to be some debate and clarification. For example, it takes a lot longer to say 'one hundred and thirty four thousand, seven hundred and sixty two', than it does to say 'six'. The children will need to agree some sort of averaging process.

● In addition, they will need to decide if the counting is continuous, without a break. Otherwise, they will need to build breaks into the time allowed. If each number takes on average three seconds, then they will take about one month to complete the task!

Activity development

● The activity requires the children to decide what information is needed and how to use it. With multi-step problems, some able children still require help to make sense of the question, sort out the information needed and to use the information appropriately.

One penny	1.5mm thick
Plastic cubes	1 000 000 1cm cubes per cubic metre
Plastic cubes	125 000 2cm cubes per cubic metre
Land's End to John O'Groats is 1500km (approx)	1500km (approx) or 2 000 000 paces

● Give out copies of photocopiable page 71. Explain that they need to decide what information is needed in order answer the question, to find that information and to write it in the space provided. Explain that they also need to write down the calculation.

● If the children need support you could look up some of the facts yourself and make them available. Some useful data is given in the table above.

Review

● It is important to go through questions and to allow the children to explain how they used the data. The answer itself is of secondary importance. In addition, ask them to explain how they found out and used approximate data, such as the average length of a pace.

Next steps
● Invite the children to think up a question to which the answer is about one million, or invent a question that involves one million. Encourage them to research and consider the data carefully, not just invent something on the spot.

● If they are struggling, ask if the oldest person on earth has been alive for a million hours. (This is a little over 114 years.)

How big is a million?

■ Each of these activities requires you to look up information and to use it to solve a problem. You are not told what information you need or what calculation to do. You need to work these out yourself.

A village has collected one million pennies to make a children's playground. How tall would the pile be if they were placed one on top of the other?

Information needed

Calculation

Answer

Could you fit one million plastic cubes into your classroom?

Information needed

Calculation

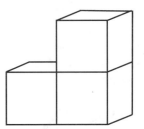

Answer

Long distance walkers sometimes walk from Land's End in Cornwall to John O'Groats in Scotland. How many paces is this?

Information needed

Calculation

Answer

Arithmagons

Activity introduction

- Display a large copy of the diagram shown below. Place two-digit number cards, such as 17, 23 and 29 in boxes A, B and C. Explain that this diagram is an arithmagon and the rules for arithmagons state that the numbers in the rectangles must be the sum of the numbers in circles either side. Ask them to calculate the numbers in boxes X, Y and Z.
- Continue by placing the numbers 6, 8 and 10 in boxes B, X and Z respectively. Say: *Can you work out the numbers in the other three boxes?* Ask them to discuss if any more work was involved this time. Repeat with more demanding numbers, such as 27, 36 and 48 in boxes A, X and Y respectively.
- If the children are happy handling negative numbers, give them the problem of A=10, X=4 and Y=7. With this calculation, some children will struggle to find Z (B=-6, C=-3 and Z=-9).

Activity development

- Place the numbers, 6, 8 and 10 in boxes X, Y and Z. Give them a moment to realise that this needs more than a simple calculation. They should work in pairs to solve the problem. Then, ask each pair to explain their method to another pair.
- The children may offer several methods of solution, although many will probably adopt a trial and improvement strategy. (In fact for some, this activity may amount to no more than a trial, followed by another trial, and so on.)
- Once a solution has been accepted (A=2, B=4, C=6), give them another set of three numbers, such as 12, 16 and 28. Put these numbers into the rectangles in any order. Allow them time to discuss and find solutions for the puzzle.
- Give out copies of photocopiable page 73. Invite the children to try the examples on their own. The third example produces values that are not whole numbers. If children need more practice with whole number examples, choose three even numbers for X, Y and Z, and make sure that the largest is not more than twice the value of the smallest.

Review

- The children report on their answers and discuss any patterns or rules they found. Some may be able to articulate a consistent method of solution. If so, invite them to explain their solution with three numbers of your choosing.

Learning objectives

(Y5) Use/apply strand:
Explore patterns, properties and relationships and propose a general statement involving numbers or shapes; identify examples for which the statement is true or false.
(Y6) Use/apply strand:
Represent and interpret sequences, patterns and relationships involving numbers; suggest and test hypotheses.

Expected prior knowledge

- Work systematically.

You will need

A large copy of the diagram shown below to display; small pieces of paper to make number cards (successive folding an A4 sheet can provide about 32 pieces of a useful size); photocopiable page 73 (one per child).

Key vocabulary

arithmagon, sum, difference

Brainteaser link

4. Arithmagon investigation

Next steps

- For most children, an algebraic method of solution is too demanding. However, some can be encouraged to explore the possibility by asking them to eliminate B and C from the diagram. Give them three numbers for X, Y and Z (three from an earlier known example will do). Ask them to replace B and C with expressions involving only A. Then ask them to use these two expressions and the value of Z to solve the puzzle.
- You can find variations on this puzzle by using a simple internet search for the word *arithmagon*.

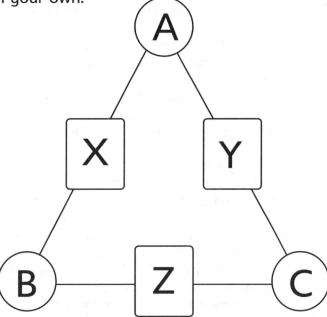

Arithmagons

◼ Solve these arithmagons when:
X = 20, Y = 32, Z = 40
X = 100, Y = 80, Z = 60
X = 10, Y = 12, Z = 15
◼ Find a relationship between X + Y + Z and A + B + C.
◼ What happens when X, Y and Z are all odd numbers?
Try some values of your own.

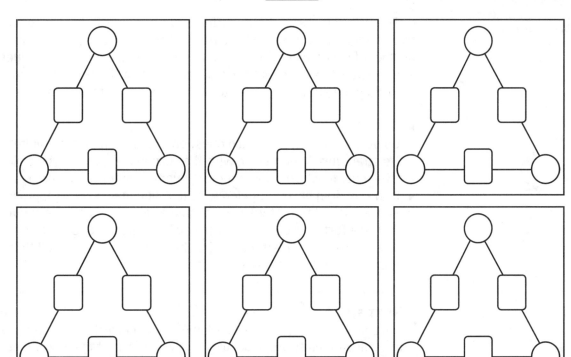

Logical loops

Activity introduction

- Draw two intersecting loops to form a simple Venn diagram. Label one of them 'cricket' and the other 'football'. Tell the following story: *Twenty teachers are surveyed to find out if they like football and cricket. Half like cricket, half like football and a quarter like neither. How many like both?*

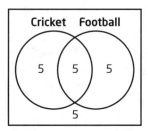

- Give the children some time to discuss the problem, to decide if they have enough information, and devise a plan to solve it. Invite them to produce a solution, either by placing cubes into appropriate spaces on the Venn diagram, or by using jottings on paper.
- The problem lends itself to trial and improvement as the children will need to distribute 15 'teachers' or cubes inside the loops and put 10 in each loop.
- Repeat the activity but alter the story so that 30 teachers are surveyed and one fifth like both, two-fifths like cricket and three-fifths like football. Ask them how many teachers don't like either sport.

Activity development

- Ask the children to close their eyes. Add a third loop to the Venn diagram and ask them to work out how many regions there are. Let them count and check, but remind them that the outside region is as important as any of the others. Give out copies of photocopiable page 75 and draw attention to the second activity. Remind them that there are eight regions and that they must use all of the information given.
- Invite the children to work alone first, then share ideas. One reason is that a child's individual train of thought can be broken by their partner's suggestions.
- The first activity uses straightforward reasoning, but is based on the use of fractions. The second activity is very demanding. To find the number of children in every region requires the use of all of the clues. The children must also make use of the fact that there are 30 children in all. If they are struggling, refer to the review below for support ideas.

Review

- Go over the answers to each question but encourage the children to share strategies. In particular, with the second activity, ask the children for the order in which they found the number for each region.
- If the children have struggled with this, you may want to approach the review in a different way. For example, you could halt the activity and offer a further clue. One which may be useful is to remind the children to use the fact there are 30 children. Another is to tell them that one of the regions has zero in it.

Learning objectives

(Y6) Use/apply strand: Solve multi-step problems, and problems involving fractions, decimals and percentages; choose and use appropriate calculation strategies at each stage, including calculator use.
(Y6) Use/apply strand: Explain reasoning and conclusions, using words, symbols or diagrams as appropriate.
(Y6) Calculate strand: Find fractions and percentages of whole-number quantities.

Expected prior knowledge

- Show confidence working with reasoning and word problems.

You will need

Photocopiable page 75; cubes or counters for the introduction.

Key vocabulary

reasoning, Venn diagram, trial and improvement

Next steps

- A demanding extension is to ask the children to make up a three-loop problem for themselves. It should be solvable, but not too easy. An early step is to determine how many clues are needed. For example, are the six clues used in the second activity on page 75 all necessary?

Logical loops

◀ A class of 30 children take part in two surveys: one about what vegetables they like, and one about their recreational activities on the previous day.
◀ Use the clues to decide how many children gave answers in each category. Write the numbers on the diagrams.

Preferred vegetables
◀ Two-thirds like carrots.
◀ One-fifth like cabbage, but not carrots.
◀ Two-fifths like both.
◀ How many like neither cabbage nor carrots?

Cabbage Carrots

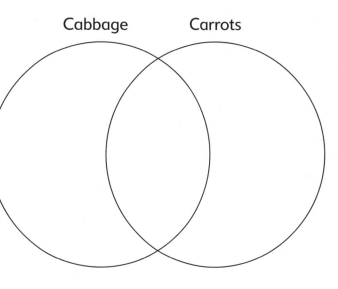

Read

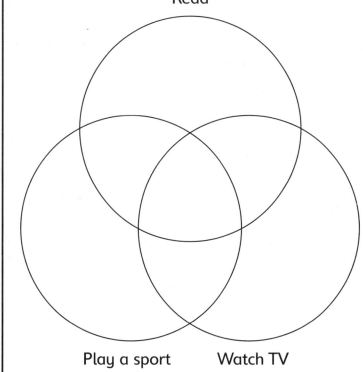

Play a sport   Watch TV

Recreational activities
◀ 18 watched TV.
◀ Two of the eight who read did neither of the other activities.
◀ For one-fifth of the children, sport was the only activity.
◀ Only 10% did all three activities.
◀ Ten of those who did sport, also watched TV.
◀ Four of the 30 children did not take part in any of the named activities.
◀ How many children read and watched TV?

You've been framed

Activity introduction

- Ask the children to draw a rectangle with a perimeter of 24cm on their squared paper. Once they have all done this, compare the results. Some may have drawn long, thin rectangles, such as 10cm by 2cm. Others may have drawn ones that are 'nearly square', such as 7cm by 5cm.
- Ask: *Which of the rectangles has the greatest area?*
- Remind them, if necessary, that a square is a special rectangle and that a 6cm by 6cm square has the greatest area.
- Repeat this activity with a perimeter of 90cm. (This time there is no square possible.) This aspect of the introductory session offers reinforcement of working with larger numbers. For example, one solution is 25cm by 20cm, with an area of 500cm^2.

Activity development

- Provide each child with photocopiable page 77 and explain that the first part of the activity is straightforward in that it relies on closed calculations. Some children may need support with converting the cost of the frame and glass into pounds.
- The question regarding a square allows a variety of approaches. While it can be done analytically, most children will adopt a trial and improvement strategy. Draw their attention to the answers from the first two parts of the question. These suggest that the square lies between the two frames already worked on.
- There is an extension at the end of the photocopiable which could be used as part of the review but which would suit two very able children working together.

Review

- If children have tackled the last activity on the photocopiable page independently, allow them to explain the results, preferably on a large whiteboard. Otherwise, explain that a spreadsheet can allow you to check a number of frames quickly. Demonstrate how to set up columns within the spreadsheet for Height, Width, Price of frame, Price of glass and Total price.

Learning objectives

(Y5) Use/apply strand: Represent a problem by identifying and recording the calculations needed to solve it; find possible solutions and confirm them in the context of the problem.

(Y6) Use/apply strand: Solve multi-step problems, and problems involving fractions, decimals and percentages, choosing and using appropriate and efficient methods at each stage, including calculator use.

Expected prior knowledge

- Recognise and tackle a complex problem involving several stages.
- Understand both area and perimeter.
- Use cm and cm^2 correctly.

You will need

Photocopiable page 77 (one per child); calculators; squared paper and pencils; computer spreadsheet program.

Key vocabulary

area, perimeter, formula

Brainteaser link

2. Domino squares

Next steps

- Explain to the children that the owner of Picture Perfect has produced a formula to work out the price in pounds of any frame, where H = height and W = width. The formula is (2H + 2W)/10 + (H × W)/100.
- Ask the children whether they think that the formula is correct.
- Ask them to use it to check their answers on photocopiable page 77.

Name _____

You've been framed

Picture Perfect is a company that makes picture frames. The price of a frame is worked out using a formula based on the perimeter of the finished frame and the area of the glass used in the frame.

Frames are priced at 10p per cm of frame and 1p per cm² of glass. The glass is assumed to be the same size as the frame.

Check that the price of this frame is correct.

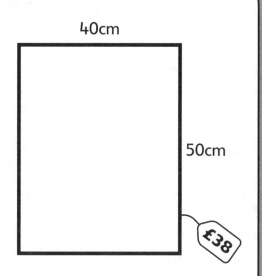

40cm

50cm

£38

Find the cost of these picture frames.

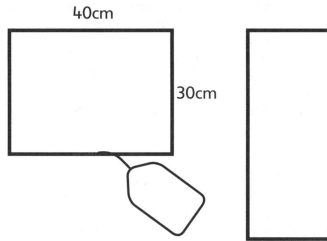

40cm

30cm

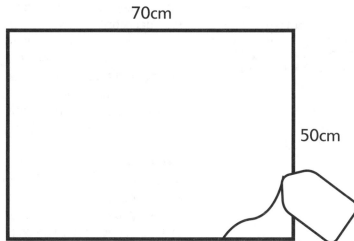

70cm

50cm

A square frame is priced at £45.
Work out the dimensions of this frame.

A picture frame is ordered which is one metre square.
What is its price?

Trains

Learning objectives
(Y6) Use/apply strand:
Solve multi-step problems;
choose and use appropriate
calculation strategies at
each stage.

**Expected prior
knowledge**
● Understanding of maps.
● Willingness to tackle a
problem without clear
directions.

You will need
Photocopiable page 79 (one
per child); paper to record
squares.

Key vocabulary
equidistant, branch line (to
denote a small railway line
attached to a larger one)

Activity introduction

● Present the children with a square labelled ABCD,
clockwise. Ask them to copy the square and mark a point
inside it which is equidistant from B and D.

● Once they have all done this, ask them to compare
solutions. Focus on solutions that are not at the centre of
the square. Ask the children how they can easily describe
all of the points that are equidistant from B and D. If necessary, lead
them to describe the diagonal AC of the square.

● Tell them that they need to mark point E such that it is equidistant
from B and D, but twice as far from A as it is from C. Allow them some
time in pairs to decode this sentence and to explore the problem. Invite
suggestions marked on a square. Point E is on the diagonal from A to C
and $^2/_3$ of the distance from A to C. Explaining all this allows the children
chance to use precise language to describe a point.

Activity development

● Hand out two copies of photocopiable page 79 to each pair. Working
in pairs will give children a chance to discuss their interpretation of the
clues. They can use one copy of the page for jottings and one for their
final decisions. Ensure that they understand the aim of the activity and
explain that they are required to
use the clues in any order they
find helpful and to keep track of
important information on the way.

● The map with stations and
distances should look like this.

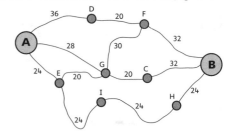

Review

● There is a good case for going through the clues one by one and
asking the children how each clue can help them. In addition, the clues
are likely to be of more use once children realise that clues can be
tackled in any order. The children need to use the final clue, together
with a number of calculations, in order to find the distance of 32km
from F to B.

● The extension activity requires some careful thought, but the
children may realise that the total distance travelled is 192km. At an
average speed of 96km per hour, the journey will take two hours. On top
of this they need to allow five minutes for each stop. There are seven
stops, (not counting the start or finish) so the total time needed is two
hours and thirty-five minutes.

> **Next steps**
> ● The extension activity can be further developed by making the
> question more demanding. An express train is introduced. It travels at
> an average speed of 128km per hour. It stops for only two minutes at
> small stations and five minutes at large ones (A and B). How long is the
> return journey?
> ● If there is time, the children can add their own stations or lines to the
> map and then create their own questions.

Trains

🔲 Three different railway lines run between two large towns, A and B. A branch line also connects three of the small stations. The only map for this railway system is shown below. But it has no station names and no distances between the stations.

🔲 Use the clues to work out the station names and the distances between them. Mark them on the map.

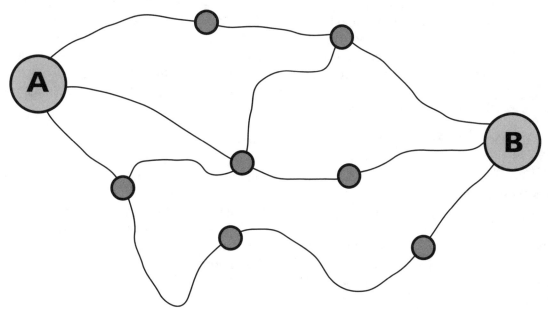

1. A train leaves station A and passes through G, before stopping at C. It travels 48km from A to C.

2. Town I is on a line with three small stations. It is 48Km from A.

3. C is 32km from B and 20km from G.

4. The small branch line goes from F to E via G and is 50km long.

5. Stations E, I and H are all equally spaced on a line between A and B.

6. Station D is 36km from A and 20km from F.

7. From G it is the same distance to C as it is to E.

8. A 'Tourist Ticket' lets you go from B to B using two of the main lines and the branch line. The total distance is 154km.

Extension

🔲 A train travels from A to B and back to A, stopping at E, I and H in both directions. It averages 96km an hour between stations and waits five minutes at each station. How long does it take from A to B and back to A?

■■SCHOLASTIC **PHOTOCOPIABLE**   🔲 **79**
www.scholastic.co.uk
50 MATHS LESSONS · AGES 9-11

Substitution codes

Activity introduction

● Write on the board the word UIJT JT B DPEF. (Each letter of the sentence, THIS IS A CODE, has been moved on one place in the alphabet.) Tell the children that this is a coded sentence in which each letter has been replaced by another letter, using a simple pattern. Allow the children time to decode the message. Ask them to show that they have decoded it by encoding the word MATHEMATICS, using the same rule. (The coded word is NBUIFNBUJDT.) Ask how they would decode a longer message, once they knew the rule.

● Ask: *What clues there are in the encoded message that might help you?* If necessary, draw their attention to the two short words encoded with JT and B. Ask them to discuss what options there are in English for one- and two-letter short words.

● Continue by asking them to encode a short sentence by moving each letter on two spaces. If they need a greater challenge, make this more demanding by suggesting a greater movement, or move straight onto the activity development.

Activity development

● Introduce the children to photocopiable page 81 (or to the discs if these have been prepared in advance). The two discs need to be cut out and the smaller one placed into the centre of the larger one. A split pin or clip joint can be used to fasten them together. The larger disc is the same size as a compact disc, so could be glued to an unwanted one.

● Ask the children to rotate the inner ring one space to the left (anti-clockwise). Ask: *What do you notice?* Return to the code used in the introduction. Ask if they can see how the discs can be used to encode the message, THIS IS A CODE.

● Explain that encoding and decoding are inverse operations like addition and subtraction. Ask them how the wheels could be used to decode the message.

● Allow the children to explore the use of the wheels and to encode and decode a range of messages. Ask them to encode messages where the wheel has been turned through other angles and to pass the messages to each other for decoding.

Review

● Collect the children's ideas together. In particular, ask them for any patterns they have spotted for deciding how far an encoded wheel has been turned. Ask why it may or may not be a good idea to use punctuation. (For example, punctuation may make a message easier to decode.)

Next steps
● Invite the children to devise their own method of encoding a message. Tell them that it is important that the inverse operation, decoding, is easy for those who know the rule but hard for those that do not.
● Use the internet to explore codes and ciphers. The author Simon Singh (**www.simonsingh.net**) has produced a lot of work on codes.

Substitution codes

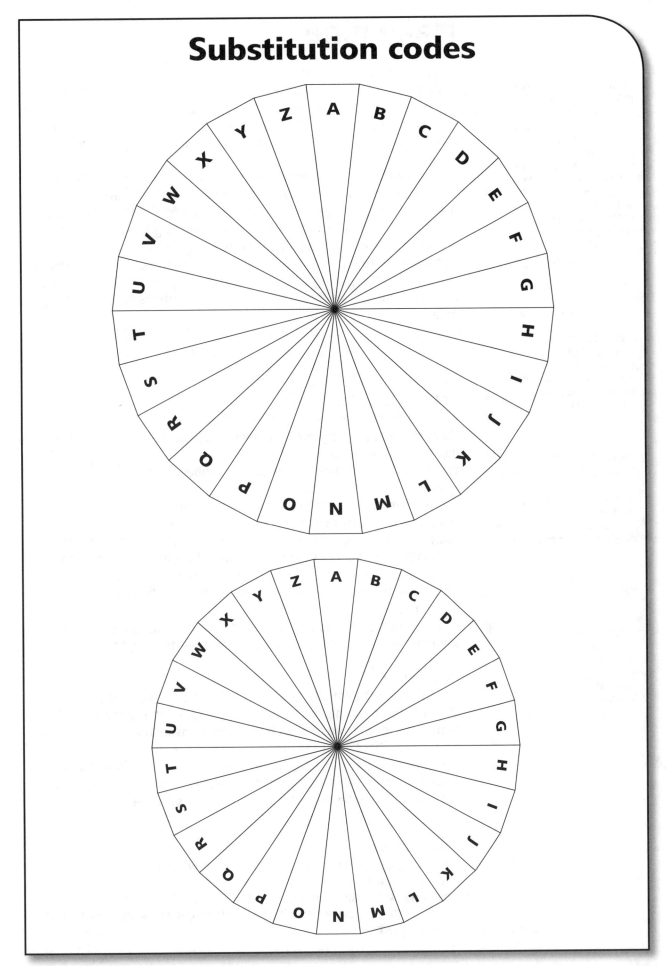

Make nine

Activity introduction

● Give each child one set of 0–9 digit cards. Ask the children to hold up three numbers that total ten. Ask them to look around at each other's solutions. Invite the children to decide whether the group has found all possible ways. (Unless this is a large group, it is unlikely that all solutions have been found.)

● Ask the children to suggest how to record the solutions to be sure that all possible answers have been found. Continue by asking them to use their strategy to record all of the possible sets of three numbers that total ten. (Some children may need prompting to use the zero.)

● Make sure they have a method of checking for duplicate solutions. Remind them that 2, 3, 5 is the same solution as 5, 2, 3. One systematic method worth exploring is to start with the lowest numbers and to work upwards. This will yield the complete set of solutions in the following order:

0, 1, 9	0, 2, 8	0, 3, 7	0, 4, 6
1, 2, 7	1, 3, 6	1, 4, 5	
2, 3, 5			

Activity development

● Show the children the diagram opposite. Invite them to find a way to place a number card in each box so that the numbers total eight in both directions. Restrict them to one set of number cards to avoid duplicate cards being used.

● Ask them to discuss any similarities between the solutions of different children. For example, two solutions are mathematically identical if one is a rotation of the other.

● Discuss this idea with the children and (if appropriate), explain the term 'mathematically distinct' in the context of the solutions found above. Ask them to explain why there is only one distinct solution to this problem.

● Introduce photocopiable page 83 and explain that there are more solutions when you allow a total of nine rather than eight.

Review

● Go through the activity and ensure that the children are satisfied that all solutions are found. Where necessary, explain that sometimes solutions appear to be distinct but on closer inspection, one of them is a rotation or reflection of the other.

● Ask them what would happen to the number of solutions if you allowed them to use a zero. Initially they may think the zero to have little value, but in fact it creates a number of additional solutions.

Learning objectives
(Y5) Use/apply strand:
Represent a problem by identifying and recording the information or calculations needed to solve it; find possible solutions and confirm them in the context of the problem.
(Y5) Use/apply strand:
Explore patterns, properties and relationships and propose a general statement involving numbers.

Expected prior knowledge
● Work systematically.
● Recognise when one pattern is a rotation or reflection of another.

You will need
Photocopiable page 83 (one per child); a set of 0–9 digit cards for each child; paper suitable for recording several copies of the diagram (see below).

Key vocabulary
systematic, sequence, pattern, mathematically distinct

Brainteaser link
9. Make 15

Next steps
● If the problem is extended so that each row and column must total ten, the number of solutions increases significantly. It becomes quite demanding to show that you have found them all. Encourage the children to work systematically and to check each new solution against those already found.

Name _____

Make nine

◗ Using number cards 1–8, place a card in each box so that the row and the column both total nine.

◗ Record your solution.

◗ Record as many different solutions as you can.

◗ On the back of this page, explain how you know you have all possible solutions.

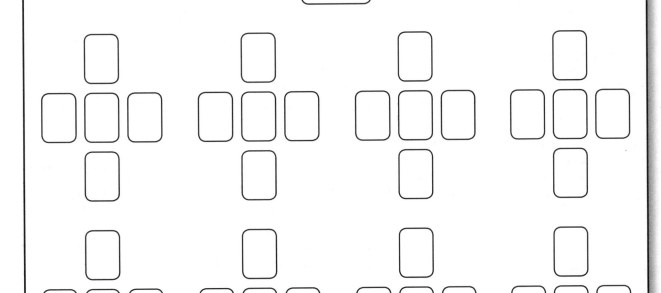

Domino puzzles

Activity introduction

● Give each pair a set of dominoes. Allow them time to become familiar with the range of numbers and pieces in the set, and realise that there are no duplicates. Explain that a domino is 'named' or 'defined' after the two numbers represented by its spots (for example, 'three/five' and so on).

● Ask: *Can each of you hold up a domino with a sum of 10?* Continue with a few more examples until they are confident.

● Ask: *Can you hold up a domino with a product of 12?* Both children in each pair can solve this as both [3, 4] and [2, 6] are in the set. Remind them that product means 'multiply', or wait until a child holds up double six, and discuss the misconception.

● Ask the children to find the product of the spots on each domino and to sort them into two piles: one for those with an even product, and one for those with an odd product. Remind them that 0 is an even number. Ask: *Why is one pile is much larger?* Discuss the formation of odd and even products.

Activity development

● Show the children the diagram on the right. Explain that six of the dominoes in the set have been arranged into a rectangle. Only the number of spots on each half of the domino can be seen, not the dominoes themselves. Ask the children to work out how the dominoes have been arranged.

4	4	2	3
2	4	4	3
3	3	2	2

● Allow time for discussion and then ask them to arrange six dominoes from their set so that the spots match this rectangle.

● Once they have a matching pattern, discuss strategies. If they are struggling, then discuss strategies to help. For example, they may notice that all of the possible dominoes that have only two, three and four on them are included. Therefore, the domino in the bottom right corner must be double two. Encourage them to reason the problem to its conclusion.

● Give out photocopiable page 85. Explain that this is a large version of the same problem. Allow them plenty of time to explore the problem and to record solutions. Some may like to have an additional copy for their workings.

Review

● Invite the children to share solutions and methods of reasoning. A large copy of photocopiable page 85 on an OHP would be useful. Colour the missing lines to make them stand out.

● This approach will allow the children to see possible lines of enquiry. One solution is shown on the right.

0	4	1	1	0	2
0	1	2	3	4	4
0	3	4	0	3	4
2	2	3	2	1	2
1	4	3	0	1	3

Next steps

● Invite the children to create their own domino puzzles. Give them a grid of squares where each square is 2.5cm or 1 inch. Suggest that they place a small set of the dominoes on the grid and then record the position of the number of spots on each half domino.

Learning objectives
(Y5) Use/apply strand:
Solve one- and two-step problems involving whole numbers and decimals and all four operations, choosing and using appropriate calculation strategies.
(Y5) Use/apply strand:
Represent a problem by identifying and recording the calculations needed to solve it; find possible solutions and confirm them in the context of the problem.
(Y6) Use/apply strand:
Tabulate systematically the information in a problem or puzzle; identify and record the steps or calculations needed to solve it, using symbols where appropriate; interpret solutions in the original context and check their accuracy.

Expected prior knowledge
● Understand dominoes.

You will need
A set of dominoes (one per pair); photocopiable page 85 (one per child), several spare copies and a large copy on an overhead projector transparency for the review.

Key vocabulary
domino, dominoes (show children the unusual formation of the plural), product

Brainteaser link
3. How many dominoes?

Domino puzzles

■ Sort and use all 15 dominoes that have a maximum of four spots on either side.

■ Place them on this board so that the number of spots matches the numbers shown.

0	4	1	1	0	2
0	1	2	3	4	4
0	3	4	0	3	4
2	2	3	2	1	2
1	4	3	0	1	3

■ Record your solutions by outlining the domino positions on these grids.

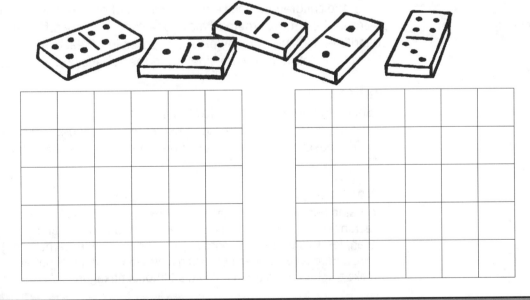

Hexagon puzzles

Activity introduction

● Give out two sets of shapes per child. Introduce the pieces from the complete set of shapes from photocopiable page 87. Make sure that the children can name each of them and describe their properties. Each hexagon is cut into an equilateral triangle, a right-angled triangle, an isosceles triangle and a rhombus.

● Ask the children to select two of the pieces to make a rectangle, two to make a right-angled triangle, two to make a trapezium and two to make an arrow head.

● Take the right-angled triangle and ask the children to use the pieces to work out its angles. This triangle is special in that its angles are 30°, 60° and 90°. The isosceles triangle has two angles of 30° and one of 120°. Indeed all of the angles which can be made are multiples of 30°. This information could be useful during the independent work.

Learning objectives
(Y5) Shape strand: Identify, visualise and describe properties of rectangles, triangles and regular polygons; use knowledge of properties to draw 2D shapes.

Expected prior knowledge
● State the names and properties of 2D shapes.

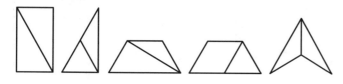

Solution

The right-angled triangle is made from an equilateral triangle and an isosceles triangle. The angles in an equilateral triangle are 60° so the bottom-left (when orientated as above) angle of the right-angled triangle must be 60°. The bottom-right angle is a right-angle (90°). The remaining angle must therefore be 30°.

Activity development

● Using just one set (two hexagons), provide the children with challenges from this list. The activities could be chosen to remind the children of a particular shape property. For example, trapeziums (trapezia) have exactly one pair of parallel sides.
    Make rectangles with 2, 3, 4, 5, 6 or 8 pieces.
    Make trapeziums (trapezia) with 2, 3, 4, 5, 6, 7 or 8 pieces.
    Make large right-angled triangles with 4, 5 or 6 pieces.
    Make large equilateral triangles with 2, 3, or 4 pieces.
    Make very large equilateral triangles with 5 or 6 pieces.
    Make a six pointed star with all of the pieces.

● Ask the children to make enlarged copies of each of the different pieces in the set. Ask them to make one copy of every different sort of quadrilateral, using as many pieces as possible for each one. They can record their solutions by drawing round their shapes on plain paper.

You will need
Shapes from photocopiable page 87 (copied on to card and cut into pieces; two sets per child).

Key vocabulary
isosceles triangle, right-angled triangle, equilateral triangle, quadrilateral, rhombus, kite, arrow head

Brainteaser link
14. Right-angled puzzle

Review

● Share and discuss recorded solutions.
● The activity could be extended to include homework and could also form the basis of a display of solutions to the various challenges.

Next steps

● Using two sets (four hexagons), invite children to make more rectangles, trapeziums (trapezia), right-angled triangles and equilateral triangles, this time using more pieces. The most able learners could investigate why squares pose such a problem, and if it is possible to make a square with the use of an additional hexagon.

Name _____

Hexagon puzzles

Lost bears

Learning objectives
(Y5) Shape strand: Read and plot coordinates in the first quadrant; recognise parallel and perpendicular lines in grids and shapes.
(Y6) Shape strand: Use coordinates in the first quadrant to draw and locate shapes.

Expected prior knowledge
● Read and plot coordinates.
● Interpret simple relationships between the x- and y-coordinates, such as $x > y$ or $x + y = 17$. The clues will be given in words rather than in symbols.

You will need
OHP or whiteboard; squared paper; photocopiable page 89 (one/two per child); coloured pens/pencils or small coloured counters/cubes (four colours per child).

Key vocabulary
coordinate, quadrant

Activity introduction
● Draw a set of axes on an OHP or whiteboard. The scales should be marked from 0 to 6 in both directions. Ask each the children to sketch a similar set of axes.
● Tell the children: *I have buried some treasure somewhere on the grid. I am going to give you some clues about the x- and y-coordinates.*
● Read out the first clue: *Where the treasure is buried, the x-coordinate is more than the y-coordinate.* Allow the children time to discuss the clue's meaning and to recognise what it means in relation to the points on the grid. Ask the children for some points which satisfy the rule. For example, (4, 3) satisfies it but (3, 4) does not. Ask the children to place crosses where the treasure *cannot* be buried.
● Read out the second clue: *The x-coordinate and the y-coordinate add up to 8.* Encourage the children to mark their page with crosses where the treasure *cannot* be buried: they should have only the points (6, 2) and (5, 3) left available.
● Ask the children to invent a clue which eliminates (5, 3) as a possible place for the treasure. Discuss the children's responses.

Activity development
● Provide each child with photocopiable page 89 and explain that the activity requires them to find three bears, which are lost on a grid. There are several clues similar to those they have just met in the introductory session. These clues will help to exclude places where the bears could not be.
● Explain to the children that it might be helpful to put small crosses on the page, or use very small counters or cubes, to mark the places or points where the bears cannot be. Choose one colour for the points which have been eliminated and three other colours for the bears.
● At the end of the activity the children are invited to create their own set of clues for a partner to solve. The children may require an additional copy of the activity sheet to work on, or you may want to prepare some blank grids for them.

Review
● Check that the children have solved each of the clues correctly and that they have found the lost bears. Baby Bear is at (2, 5), Mummy Bear is at (4, 5), and Daddy Bear is at (8, 9).
● Ask the children to explain how they used the clues. In particular, ask them to explain which of the clues was the most helpful.

Next steps
● At the end of the activity children are invited to hide their own bears and to set clues. This can be extended to all four quadrants, using squared or graph paper.
● Activity 35, 'Treasure hunt', is a demanding development of the mathematical ideas encountered in this activity.

Lost bears

◼ There are three bears, Mummy, Daddy and Baby, lost in the grid below. Each is standing on a pair of whole-number coordinates.

◼ Use the clues to find and mark them with the bears' names.

Clues

Baby Bear is 2 years old.

The *x*-coordinate of each of the bears is less than 9.

The *y*-coordinate of Baby Bear is 3 more than the bear's age in years.

The sum of the *x*- and *y*-coordinates of Mummy Bear is a multiple of 3.

The *y*-coordinate of each of the bears is more than the *x*-coordinate.

The *x*-coordinate of Mummy Bear is 2 more than the *x*-coordinate of Baby Bear.

The *y*-coordinate of Daddy Bear is 4 more than the *y*-coordinate of Mummy Bear.

The sum of the *x*- and *y*-coordinates for Daddy Bear is 17.

The *x*-coordinate of Daddy Bear is a multiple of 4.

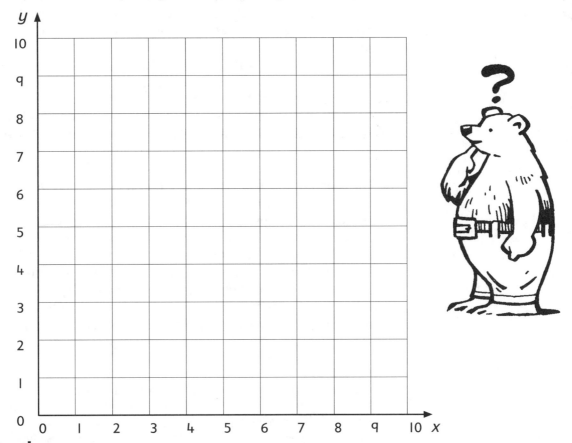

Extension

◼ Hide three bears on a grid and make up a set of clues of your own. Give them to a partner to solve. Hint: When making clues, it is easier to mark where the bears are first, and then make up clues to fit.

Missing corners

Activity introduction

- On an OHP or whiteboard, draw and number some axes from -5 to 5 in both the x and y directions. Draw and label the points A(-3, -3), B(-3, 4) and C(4, 4).
- Tell the children that these three points are three corners of a square. Ask: *What are the coordinates of the fourth corner?* Encourage them to explain their reasoning. Ask: *What is the length of a side of the square?*
- Repeat the activity with the points A(2, -2), B(-1, 1) and C(2, 4). Ask the children to explain how they know this is a square. Discuss with the children the use of correct terminology. Try to discourage them from using terms such as 'diamond' to describe the shape.
- Finally, repeat the activity with points A(-2, -4), B(-3, 1) and C(2, 2). The orientation of this square makes the task more demanding.

Activity development

- Provide each child with photocopiable page 91 and a sheet of squared paper for experimentation. Make sure the children understand the expectations of the activity. Some children may find the orientation of the squares too demanding. You might like to suggest that they use the corner of the squared paper as a guide to searching for right angles. They can line up two points with one of them at a corner of the page. The adjacent edge of the paper will pass through the third corner of the square.
- If the children need further help, tell them that the square in the bottom-right quadrant is complete. In addition, there is a square in the first quadrant (top right) which is straightforward.
- As children finish, a simple checking device is to see whether they have correctly identified the point (2, 1) as the only one not used.

Review

- The children should be able to see that their solutions are correct, once the squares are drawn in. The final problem is worth exploring with the children during the review.
- Draw a grid on an OHP or whiteboard and mark on it the points from the final stage of the activity. These are A(0, -7), B(-3, 3) and C(7, 6). Invite the children to explain how they found the coordinates of the missing corner. The position of the missing point is D(10, -4). Since the position is off the page, there is a need to use reasoning, although some children may have opted to draw larger axes to solve the problem.

Next steps

- To extend the children's understanding, and to prepare the way for future work on vectors, encourage the children to explain their solution to the final problem using a 'journey' from one point to another. The number of squares moved horizontally or vertically always involves the numbers 10 and 3 (which can be seen clearly in the journey from A to B). This method can be used to solve all of the examples in the activity.

Learning objectives
(Y6/Y7) Shape strand: Find coordinates of points determined by geometric information.

Expected prior knowledge
- Read and write coordinate notation for points in all four quadrants.

You will need
OHP or whiteboard; photocopiable page 91 (one per child); squared paper (one sheet per child).

Key vocabulary
axis, coordinate, quadrant

Missing corners

◢ On this grid there are at least five hidden squares. Only one of them has all four corners showing. The other four have a corner missing.

◢ Can you find the squares and draw them in? Hint: Each point could be a corner for more than one square.

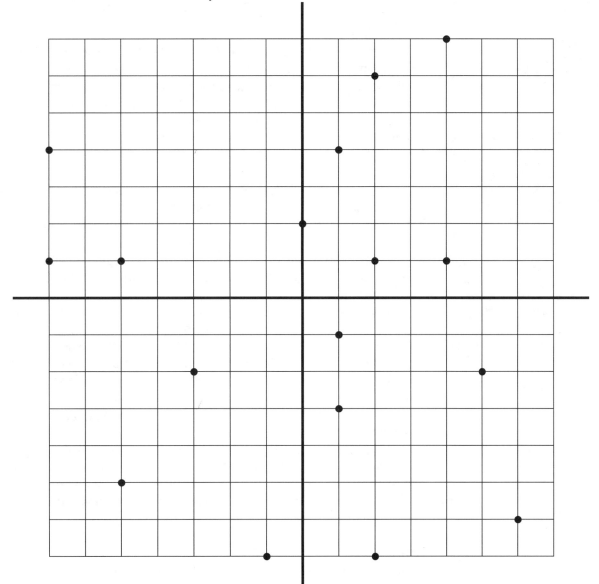

◢ One of the points on the grid above has not been used. Write down its coordinates.

◢ Another square, ABCD, is to be added to the grid. It has coordinates A(0, –7), B(–3, 3), C(7, 6).

◢ Find the coordinates of D. Try to find the coordinates by reasoning rather than by drawing.

Quadrilateral properties

Activity introduction

- Draw the grid below on an OHP or whiteboard. Make sure there is room in each box to draw a triangle.
- Explain to the children that each cell contains a triangle with the properties

	No right angles	One right angle
Scalene		
Isosceles		
Equilateral		

of both the row and column label. Ask the children to discuss with a partner what sort of triangle needs to go in each cell.
- Record the results of the discussion by drawing the children's suggestions in the appropriate box. Ask the children to justify their choice of triangle by referring to the properties of the shape. Ask them to explain why there is no triangle in one of the boxes.

Activity development

- Provide each child with photocopiable page 93 and explain that they are going to do the same sort of activity but this time with quadrilaterals. The properties used are the number of right angles and the number of parallel sides (taken in pairs).
- Make sure the children are happy with the properties of parallel lines before they begin. Emphasise that some of the boxes can contain more than one shape.
- Encourage the children to find versions of the kite, arrow head and trapezium which include right angles. You may need to remind them of the properties of each of these before they begin. One point to note is that there is a small difference between a triangle and a quadrilateral in the way that the word 'scalene' is used. In relation to triangles it means that the three sides are of different lengths. In relation to quadrilaterals it means that there are no special properties: a scalene quadrilateral may have two sides the same.
- Some of the cells are easy to fill but others are more challenging. It is worth noting that the definition of a trapezium is a quadrilateral with one pair of parallel sides. It may or may not have a right angle. A kite may have none, one or two right angles. These variations allow several of the cells to be filled.

Review

- Display a large version of the table from photocopiable page 93. Invite the children to offer suggestions for each cell. If a cell has no shape in it, ask the children to explain why.

Next steps

- Create a table similar to the one used in the activity. The titles for the four rows should be changed to: 'No equal sides', 'Two equal sides', 'Three equal sides' and 'Four equal sides'. This will allow a wide range of additional shapes to be made.

Learning objectives
(Y6) Shape strand: Describe, identify and visualise parallel and perpendicular edges or faces; use these properties to classify 2D shapes.

Expected prior knowledge
- Name quadrilaterals and list their basic properties.

You will need
OHP or whiteboard; photocopiable page 93 (one per child); plain paper (per child); enlarged version of the table on photocopiable page 93.

Key vocabulary
square, rectangle, parallelogram, trapezium, kite, rhombus, arrow head, scalene, quadrilateral, isosceles, equilateral

Brainteaser links
19. Hidden shapes

Quadrilateral properties

◗ Make sure that you know the properties of each of the quadrilaterals. These are; square, rectangle, trapezium, kite, rhombus, arrow head, parallelogram, scalene quadrilateral.

◗ Write the name of a shape and draw an accurate diagram of it in the correct cell. If it is impossible to make a shape with the correct properties leave the cell empty.

	No parallel sides	One pair of parallel sides	Two pairs of parallel sides
No right angles			
One right angle			
Two right angles			
Four right angles			

Symmetrical squares

Activity introduction

● Draw a six by six grid of squares on a large sheet of paper, an OHP or an interactive whiteboard.

● Label the squares on the grid with letters across the bottom and numbers up the side. In this way a whole square, such as D3, can be referenced, rather like chess notation or the squares on a street map.

● Shade (or cover) a few of the squares. Explain to the children how the notation for each square is to be used and then tell them that they must decide which other squares need to be shaded if the whole grid of squares is to have a vertical line of symmetry. Invite suggestions for squares to be shaded.

● Repeat the activity, first for a horizontal line of symmetry and then for two lines of symmetry.

● Repeat the activity twice more, but ask first for two-fold rotational symmetry and then for four-fold rotational symmetry.

Activity development

● Provide each child with photocopiable page 95 and explain to the class that they must shade exactly 12 squares on each grid to give the symmetry property shown. The first three involve only line symmetry and should be straightforward; the fourth and fifth are more demanding.

● The final grid is impossible. You may want to hint at this or to leave the children to work it out for themselves. When the fact that it is impossible has been established, invite the children to explain why this is so.

● If the children require further challenge, ask them to find the minimum number of squares which must be shaded in each of the grids in order to meet the symmetry property shown.

Review

● Share selected solutions to each grid with the whole group, especially any which are unusual. If you have a grid with the labelling system used in the introduction available, the children can give their solutions using the letter-number notation.

● When you reach the final grid, give the children time to explain why it is impossible. Encourage explanations which show that if you meet the rotational symmetry requirements you are forced to produce a shape with either no lines of symmetry or four lines of symmetry.

Next steps
● On triangular grid paper (equilateral triangles), draw a regular hexagon. Explore the different lines of symmetry and the different orders of rotational symmetry which are possible when small triangles are shaded.

Learning objectives
(Y6) Shape strand:
Visualise and draw on grids of different types where a shape will be after reflection or after rotation through 90° or 180° about its centre or one of its vertices.

Expected prior knowledge
● Understand line symmetry and rotational symmetry, when used to describe a shape.

You will need
Large sheet of paper, OHP or interactive whiteboard; photocopiable page 95 (one per child); triangular grid paper (for the 'Next steps activity').

Key vocabulary
two-fold (and four-fold) rotational symmetry, axis of line symmetry, regular

Symmetrical squares

 Shade exactly 12 squares in each diagram so that the grid of shaded squares has the correct symmetry property. Try to do it in an interesting or unusual way.

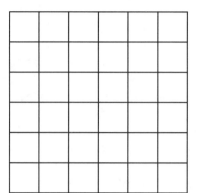

Exactly one line of symmetry

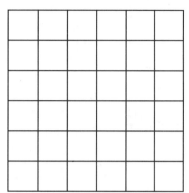

Exactly two lines of symmetry

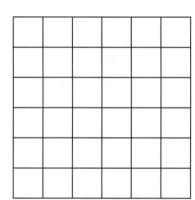

Exactly four lines of symmetry

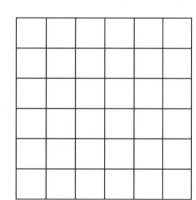

Two-fold rotational symmetry, but no line symmetry

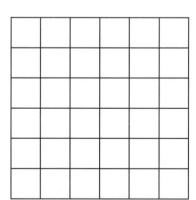

Four-fold rotational symmetry, but no line symmetry

Four-fold rotational symmetry and exactly one line of symmetry

Treasure hunt

Learning objectives
(Y6) Shape strand: Use coordinates in the first quadrant to draw and locate shapes.
(Y7) Shape strand: Find coordinates of points determined by geometric information.

Expected prior knowledge
● Read and plot coordinates in the first quadrant.
● Interpret simple relationships between the x- and y-coordinate, such as $x > y$, $x + y = 12$ or $x = 2y$.

You will need
OHP or interactive whiteboard; photocopiable page 97 (one per child); squared paper for experimentation and extension.

Key vocabulary
coordinate, greater than, less than, inequality, equation

Activity introduction

● On an OHP or interactive whiteboard, draw a set of axes marked from 0 to 10 in both directions. Explain: *I have buried three lots of treasure, marked A, B and C, somewhere on the grid. I am going to give you some clues about the x- and y-coordinates.*

Clues for A: $x + y = 12$ $x = 2y$
Clues for B: $x - y = 4$ $x + y = 10$
Clues for C: $x > y$ $x + y = 6$ $x - y = 2$

● Discuss each clue, making sure the children understand the meaning of each of the terms, such as $x = 2y$. Invite them to offer possible solutions to each clue. One possibility with less confident learners is to make a list of pairs of numbers that satisfy each part of a clue; these can then be compared and the pair of numbers (or coordinates) in both lists identified.

● Some children may need a little support interpreting relationships such as $x = 2y$. Say: *Give me a pair of numbers for x and y such that the x value is twice the y value.* Pairs of numbers such as (2, 1), (4, 2), (12, 6) should be forthcoming. Monitor the children's responses to check that they do not confuse $x = 2y$ with $y = 2x$.

Solution

A is at (8, 4), B is at (7, 3) and C is at (4, 2).

Activity development

● Give out photocopiable page 97 and explain that the activity requires them to find treasure that is hidden rather more carefully. There are four clues similar to those they have met already. These clues will produce coordinates that are the four corners of a square. However, to find the location of the treasure, the children must draw the diagonals of the square and find the intersection.

● If they need additional support, tell them that the square is rotated.

● At the end of the activity the children are invited to create their own Treasure hunt.

Solution

A(2, 10), B(10, 12), C(12, 4) D(4, 2). Diagonals intersect at the point (7, 7).

Review

● Check that the children have solved each of the clues correctly and that they have a square. They may have been surprised to find that the square is rotated, making the activity more challenging.

Next steps
● Extend the ideas developed here to all four quadrants. If the children are confident, then they can bury their own treasure. Alternatively, draw some axes from −6 to 6 in both directions and highlight a point, such as (−3, 5). Ask them to give you an inequality or an equation for which $x = -3$ or $y = 5$ is the solution.

● The mathematical principles of working in all four quadrants are the same but children usually find the transition to negative coordinates daunting. They may need time to come to terms with inequalities such as $x > -3$, and the fact that both −2 and 0 satisfy this inequality.

Treasure hunt

■ Some treasure has been buried at a point on the grid. To find it you must solve the clues. Each set of clues will give you the coordinates of a corner of the square ABCD. The treasure is at the intersection of the diagonals of this square. Mark each corner with the letter from the clue and then draw the square. Draw the diagonals and find where the treasure is buried.

Clues for point A	**Clues for point B**	**Clues for point C**	**Clues for point D**
1 $x + y = 12$	**1** $x > 9$	**1** $x = 3y$	**1** $x = 2y$
2 $y = x + 8$	**2** $y > 10$	**2** $x + y = 16$	**2** $x + y = 6$
	3 $y - x = 2$		

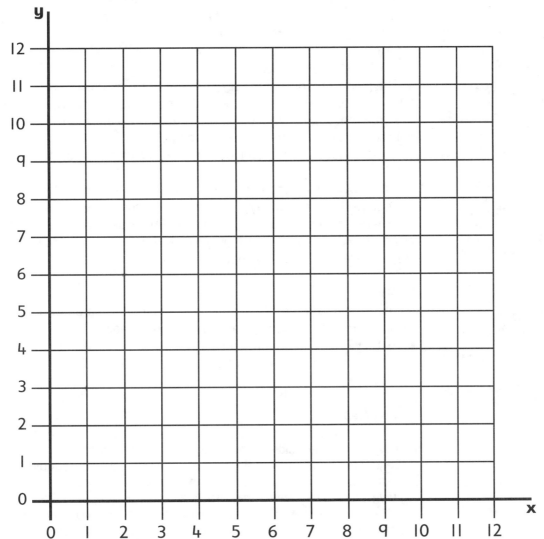

Extension

On squared paper, work out where your treasure is buried and devise a set of clues for a partner to solve. Hint: It is easier to mark the treasure and the square first and then write the clues for the coordinates.

Diagonals

Activity introduction

Number of People	Number of Crackers
2	1
3	3
4	6
5	10
6	15

- Offer the children a story context for pulling crackers. For example: *At some parties there are enough crackers for everyone to have one each. But at my party I want everyone to pull a cracker with everyone else. How many crackers do I need?* If there are (for example) two people, including you, then only one cracker is needed. Ask: *How many are needed for three people?*
- Continue by asking how many crackers are needed for four people. Suggest that they create a diagram to help or lay out pencils to represent the crackers. While they discuss the problem, make a table like the one on the right of the results (up to four) for them to see.
- Continue the problem for five people and add the number to the table. Ask: *How many crackers are needed for six people?*
- Invite them to describe any patterns they see. Some children may have seen the triangle numbers before and will recognise the pattern. Ask: *How does the pattern continue?*

Activity development

- The main activity seems very different but the number patterns that arise have strong connections with the introduction. Ask the children to describe the diagonal of a polygon. (They may be used to the idea that only squares or rectangles have diagonals.)
- Explain that diagonals can join any two vertices of a polygon, providing that they are not adjacent.
- Ask: *How many diagonals does a square have?* Continue by asking them to work out how many diagonals a pentagon has, without drawing it.
- Give out copies of photocopiable page 99. Explain that they must find all possible diagonals for each polygon, and that they need to work systematically, joining diagonals with a ruler.

Review

- The main purpose of the review is to allow the children to check the results in their table. The decagon has 35 diagonals.
- As they have had to draw the decagon themselves, some children may have missed some diagonals.

Learning objectives
(Y6) Use/apply strand: Tabulate systematically the information in a problem or puzzle; identify and record the steps or calculations needed to solve it, using symbols where appropriate; interpret solutions in the original context and check their accuracy.
(Y6) Shape strand: Make and draw shapes with increasing accuracy and apply knowledge of their properties.

Expected prior knowledge
- Work independently on and extended problem.
- Understand how to search for and use a pattern found during an investigation.

You will need
Long pencils or tubes to simulate Christmas crackers; a ruler; photocopiable page 99 (one per child); a decagon for the children to draw round towards the end of the main activity.

Key vocabulary
pentagon, hexagon, heptagon, octagon, nonagon, decagon, triangle numbers, vertex, vertices, adjacent

Next steps
- Ask: *Can you predict the number of diagonals needed for larger polygons?* Those children who have already tackled the Lesson 8 'Sequences 2' (see page 42) may suggest using a difference table. This method will work well with predicting the number of diagonals for polygons with between 11 and 15 sides.
- However, the most able should be capable of finding a relationship between the two columns of the table. Invite them to look closely at how the diagonals are formed. To find the number of diagonals that meet at each vertex, they need to realise that it is not possible to join a diagonal to an adjacent vertex or to itself. Therefore, they need to subtract 3 from the number of vertices. They can do this for each vertex. As each diagonal has two ends, they must divide the total they get by 2. If there are n vertices, then there will be $n(n-3)/2$ diagonals.

Name _____

Diagonals

1. Draw all the possible diagonals on each of these polygons. Transfer your results into the table below.

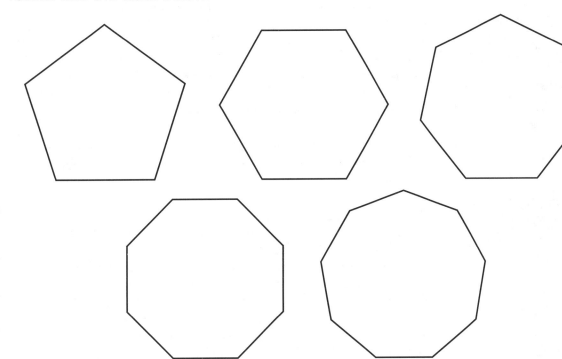

Number of sides	Number of diagonals
3	
4	
5	
6	
7	
8	
9	
10	

2. Use your results to predict the number of diagonals on a ten sided polygon (a decagon). Use the back of this page to draw a decagon and check if your prediction is correct

Pick's theorem

Learning objectives
(Y6) Use/apply strand:
(Represent a problem)
identify and record the
steps and calculations
needed to solve it, using
symbols where appropriate;
interpret solutions in the
original context and check
their accuracy.
(Y6) Shape strand: Make
and draw shapes with
increasing accuracy and
apply knowledge of their
properties.

Expected prior knowledge
● Calculate and measure
the area of squares and
parts of a square.

You will need
Photocopiable 101 (one per
child); square dotty paper
for exploration; geoboards if
available (boards with a
lattice of spikes or nails
arranged in squares - rubber
bands are stretched around
the nails to make shapes).

Key vocabulary
area, boundary, theorem

Brainteaser links
18. The missing square

Activity introduction
● On a geoboard, (or square dotty paper if boards are not available), create the shape shown on the right. Ask the children to calculate the area of the shape. You may like to give them a copy of this shape, or let them draw it on dotty paper.

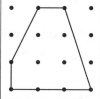

● Discuss the best way to break the shape into smaller parts to make it easier to calculate the area. The area has four whole squares and two triangles. One of triangles has an area of 1 and the other has an area of 1.5. This gives a total area of 6.5. Explain to the children that we are not interested in the units used to measure the area, only its value.
● Invite the children to draw another shape with the same area, but using a different arrangement of dots. Record several of these for the children to see.

Activity development
● Draw the children's attention to one way of recording information about this shape. It has four unused dots inside; we record this as I = 4. It has seven dots on its boundary; we record this as B = 7. We could say that for this shape, A (area) = 6.5, I = 4 and B = 7. Ask the children for the values of A, I and B for a square drawn on four adjacent dots in a square. They should find that A = 1, I = 0 and B = 4.
● Introduce them to photocopiable page 101. Explain that in 1899 a mathematician called Georg Pick published an excellent way to calculate the area of a shape drawn on a lattice of squares. Ask the children to discover Pick's formula for themselves, by drawing lots of diagrams and recording the information on each one. If they need more information, make square dotty paper available for additional recording.

Review
● Allow the children to share their conjectures about Pick's formula. Remind them that any formula they have must satisfy all shapes drawn on a grid. Re-introduce the one used in the introduction, and use it as a test. Any formulae that the children offer must work for this shape. It may be necessary to work as a collective with all the shapes the children have, and an enlarged table of results. The formula the children are looking for is A = I + B/2 - 1. In words this can be read as: the area is found by adding the inside dots to half of those on the boundary, and subtracting 1.

Next steps
● This is a very good activity to explore using an interactive whiteboard and software that allows you to alter the shape easily. You may like to look at this approach yourself, or invite some children to run it as a demonstration for others. This approach also allows you to look at a lot of cases quite quickly. For example, some insight into the problem can be gained by keeping the number of dots inside zero.

Pick's theorem

1. Here are some shapes. For each shape, record the number of dots on the inside (I), the boundary (B) and the overall area (A) in the table.

2. Make some shapes of your own and add them to the table.

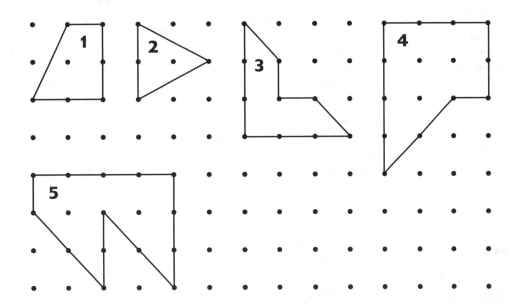

Shape	Dots Inside I	Dots on boundary B	Area of shape A
1			
2			
3			
4			
5			
6			
7			

3. Can you find a formula that lets you calculate A, if you know I and B?

Euler's formula

Activity introduction

● Give the children access to a variety of polygons. Tell them they are going to make solids, and record their properties. Make sure they understand the terms 'vertex' and 'vertices'. Ask them to make a simple solid that has exactly ten vertices.

● Then ask them to discuss with other pairs, first to check that every solid has ten vertices, then to see if the solids all have the same number of faces and edges. There will probably be solids with a range of different vertices, to make the debate worthwhile.

● Ask one of each pair to make a solid with as few pieces as possible but exactly ten vertices. The other child makes a solid with as many pieces as possible but exactly ten vertices. Ask the children to examine each other's solids, and note the number of faces or edges each has. Invite them to offer any informal comments they notice. For example, it is possible to find ten vertices in a shape made from a lot of small polygons, but it is also possible to use a few larger ones. A good solid to illustrate the first property is the pentagonal prism (which has seven faces) while a solid five-pointed star (having 12 faces) illustrates the second property well.

Activity development

● Give out copies of photocopiable page 103 and discuss the objectives of the activity. The children can make any simple solid, providing it is closed. Firstly, make a solid with the children and collectively count faces, vertices and edges. The table contains example information for a cube, but a cube does not present demands when counting. A good solid to test is a dodecahedron. You should find that $F=12$, $V=20$ and $E=32$.

● The formula the children are looking for relates the number of vertices (V), faces (F), and edges (E) for all simple closed solids. It was first published by the Swiss mathematician, Leonhard Euler (pronounced 'oiler') in the seventeenth century. The formula is $F + V - E = 2$

Review

● Discuss the children's attempts to find relationships between the number of faces, edges and vertices. This could prove difficult if the children have counted incorrectly. Check this mentally by asking a child for the results of one of their solids. Quickly apply the formula to the given results. If $F + V - E$ does not give 2, then there is a miscount.

● Stretch their imagination by explaining that this formula will work for every closed solid, no matter how complicated. If there is time, they could try a very large or complex shape as a test. Make sure that it is a closed solid with all pieces in place. They may need help with counting. Use small sticky notes to keep track of the process.

Learning objectives
(Y5) Shape strand: Identify, visualise and describe properties of regular polygons and 3D solids.
(Y6) Shape strand: Describe, identify and visualise parallel and perpendicular edges or faces; use these properties to classify 3D solids.
(Y6) Shape strand: Make and draw shapes with increasing accuracy and apply knowledge of their properties.

Expected prior knowledge
● Know the names and basic properties of regular polygons.

You will need
Photocopiable page 103 (one per pair); an array of regular polygons that clip together to make solids (such as Polydron™); small sticky notes.

Key vocabulary
polygon, triangle, square, pentagon, hexagon, octagon, regular, vertex, vertices, face, edge

Next steps
● It is possible to construct a solid that does not obey Euler's Formula. To do so, you need to make one with a hole through it, like a ring doughnut. The simplest way is to use lots of equilateral triangles or lots of squares. It is a demanding task, but for those who enjoy this sort of challenge, the reward is a solid that satisfies the formula $F + V - E = 0$.

Euler's formula

You will need to use lots of regular polygons that can be clipped together.

Construction rules:

- ◢ Make a simple solid.
- ◢ Record the number of faces, vertices and edges in the table.
- ◢ If you can also name the solid, write this in the table.

A cube has been done for you.

Solid	Number of faces	Number of vertices	Number of edges
Cube	6	8	12

◢ Can you find a simple relationship between the numbers in these columns?

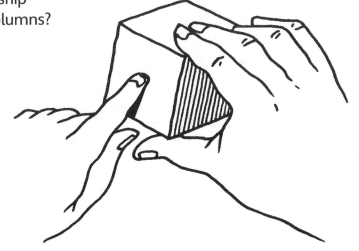

Platonic solids

Learning objectives
(Y5) Shape strand: Identify, visualise and describe properties of regular polygons and 3D solids.
(Y6) Shape strand: Describe, identify and visualise parallel and perpendicular edges or faces and use these properties to classify 3D solids.
(Y6) Shape strand: Make and draw shapes with increasing accuracy and apply knowledge of their properties.

Expected prior knowledge
● Know the names and basic properties of regular polygons.

You will need
Photocopiable page 105 (one per pair); regular polygons that clip together to make solids (such as Polydron™).

Key vocabulary
polygon, triangle, square, pentagon, hexagon, Platonic (Plato), regular, plane of symmetry, axis of rotational symmetry, vertex, face, edge, tessellation

Activity introduction
● Give the children access to lots of polygons and ask them to make a simple solid using between eight and ten shapes. Once they have completed this, ask them to describe any properties of their solid to their partners or neighbours. Encourage them to use terms such as face, vertex, edge and symmetry.
● While they do this, identify any solids that allow you to illustrate properties such as symmetry. A solid will have a plane of symmetry or an axis of rotational symmetry, rather than a line of symmetry. Define a regular polygon (that is a polygon with equal edges and equal angles) and then repeat the task, but this time, insist that all constructed polygons are regular.
● Ask the children to make a cube using the polygons. Invite them to identify the properties of the solid. Draw their attention to the property that at each vertex (corner) of the cube, three squares meet. Ask them to make a solid in which four squares meet at each vertex.
● Some children will probably make a mat of squares and try to fold it to make a solid. After a while, invite them to explain why it is impossible to do this. If four squares meet at every vertex, there is a tessellation or tiling pattern of squares.
● Sum up the introduction by drawing the children's attention to the fact that a cube is made from one sort of regular polygon, the square, and that each vertex is the same.

Activity development
● Tell the children that the remainder of the activity is about making other solids in which there is only one sort of regular polygon, and each vertex is the same. Give out photocopiable page 105 and encourage them to work on their own, but to collaborate to test ideas.

Review
● The activity encourages the children to use clues and discussion to sort out which solid is which, and to complete the table. The first part of each word offers a clue to the number of shapes used, although few children will be familiar with the Greek word 'icosi' meaning 20.
● Draw the children's attention to the final column. For the solids involving squares and pentagons, there is only one arrangement - three polygons meet at each vertex. However, for triangles there are three arrangements with three, four and five polygons respectively.
● Conclude by explaining the context of the activity. The last of these solids, the icosahedron, is unfortunately not mentioned in the Primary National Strategy. However, the set of solids, named after Plato, underpins most of solid geometry and architecture.

> ### Next steps
> ● Invite the children to investigate the family of solids that can be constructed if the rules are relaxed. For example, what happens if more than one polygon can be used but we still insist that each vertex is the same?

Platonic solids

You will need to use lots of regular polygons that can be clipped together.
Construction rules:
◀ Each solid is made from regular polygons.
◀ Each solid is made from just one sort of polygon.
◀ For each solid, every vertex is the same.
Here are pictures of all five of the solids it is possible to make using these rules.

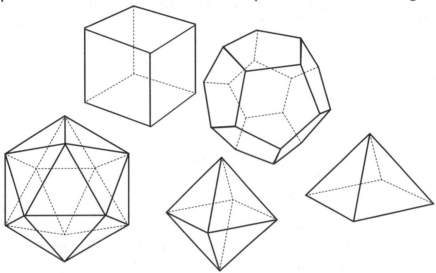

1. Use the pictures and the first part of each name to help you make the solids and complete the table.

Solid	Shape used	Number of shapes	Number at each vertex
Cube	Square	6	3
Dodecahedron			
Tetrahedron			
Octahedron			
Icosahedron			

2. Explain why you cannot make a solid in which six triangles meet at each vertex.

_____

_____

Crossing the country

Learning objectives
(Y5) Use/apply strand:
Explain reasoning, using diagrams, graphs and text.
(Y5) Measure strand: Read timetables and time using 24-hour clock notation.

Expected prior knowledge
● Use a 24-hour clock and read a railway timetable.
● Calculate elapsed time from a timetable.
● Know that speed is calculated by dividing distance travelled by time elapsed.
● Calculate an average speed.

You will need
OHP or whiteboard; photocopiable page 107 (one per pair); calculators (optional); enlarged version of photocopiable page 107.

Key vocabulary
timetable, time elapsed, average speed

Activity introduction
● Using an OHP or whiteboard, present the children with the section of a railway timetable shown below, with the times shaded in grey missing. Explain what the timetable is telling us. Ask them to calculate the approximate time taken between the two stations, noting that the journey times are not constant.
● Invite the children to suggest what the missing times might be and explain their reasoning. Two possible times are shown. There is no one correct answer: much of the value of this exercise lies in the discussion.
● Continue the activity and discussion, using the section of a timetable for the return journey, shown below.

Nottingham	09.12	10.36	09.40	12.35	13.55
Chesterfield	09.52	11.13	12.20	13.17	14.30

Chesterfield	10.00	11.15	12.23		
Nottingham				15.00	16.05

Activity development
● Tell the children that it is 50km from Chesterfield to Nottingham. Invite discussion about how to calculate the speed of the train, using the information given. Typically the train takes less than 50 minutes to travel 50km. It is therefore travelling at rather more than 1km a minute, or just over 60km per hour. If calculators are available then a more precise measure can be made.
● Provide each child with photocopiable page 107 and ask them to work in pairs to complete the sheet. Point out that the questions do not always have precise answers. Explain that they should make a good estimate when necessary and discuss their estimates with their partners.

Review
● If possible, display an enlarged version of the timetable from photocopiable page 107 on an OHP or whiteboard. Invite children to offer solutions to each of the questions. Note that the final question has no one correct answer. Encourage the children to offer their reasoning for each entry, and allow discussion of alternative views.
● In answer to the extension question, at the time of publication the best journey from Exeter to Manchester Piccadilly, arriving in time to catch the 15.37 train, is as follows:
Depart Exeter St David's at 10.23
Arrive Birmingham New Street at 12.59 (where you change on to a Manchester train)
Depart Birmingham New Street at 13.18
Arrive Manchester Piccadilly at 15.02

Next steps
● Children can use the internet to explore other journeys across the country. For example, ask them to find different routes and journey times from where they live to London, Birmingham or Manchester.

Crossing the country

LESSON 40   Name _____

Here is part of a timetable which is being considered for trains between Norwich and Liverpool. Study it carefully and then try to answer the questions below.

Norwich				12.52	13.49		15.53	16.57	18.45	19.30	20.51		
Thetford				13.19	14.16		16.20	17.24	19.12	19.57	21.18		
Ely				13.49	14.47		17.51		19.46	20.22	21.46		
Peterborough				14.28	15.25		17.15	18.30	20.25	20.55	22.20		
Grantham				14.57	15.58		17.49	19.05	21.00		22.55		
Nottingham	09.12	10.36	11.45	12.35	13.33	14.38	15.34	16.44	17.32	18.33	19.45	21.40	22.10	23.35
Chesterfield	09.52	11.13	12.20	13.17	14.17	15.16	16.16	17.20	18.12	19.13	20.15	22.10
Sheffield	10.15	11.37	12.39	13.37	14.37	15.35	16.36	17.42	18.35	19.25	20.35
Stockport	11.22	12.24	13.25	14.23	15.33	16.23	17.23	18.26	19.23	20.23	21.17
Manchester Piccadilly	11.37	12.37	13.37	14.37	15.37	16.37	17.37	18.37	19.37	20.32	21.28
Liverpool Lime Street	12.22	14.25	15.24	16.25	17.25	18.25	19.25	20.25

Liverpool Lime Street	12.00
Manchester Piccadilly	
Stockport	
Sheffield	
Chesterfield	
Nottingham	

■ How long does the first train from Nottingham take to reach Liverpool Lime Street?

■ What is the shortest journey time from Nottingham to Liverpool Lime Street?

■ The distance from Grantham to Nottingham is 40km. Use the timetable to calculate the average speed between these two places.

■ Use the times between stations to complete this section of the return journey from Liverpool Lime Street to Nottingham.

■ There is a proposal to extend the train service. The empty white boxes in the timetable above represent when the extended service will run. Use other entries in the timetable to estimate suitable times for the new service. Fill your estimates into the boxes.

Extension

I want to travel by train from Exeter to meet the 15.37 at Manchester Piccadilly.

■ Use the internet to find the times and details of my best journey.

SCHOLASTIC PHOTOCOPIABLE
www.scholastic.co.uk

107
50 MATHS LESSONS • AGES 9–11

Paper sizes

Activity introduction

● Tell the children that they are going to find out how many sheets of A4 paper are needed to cover a table. Ask the children to estimate how many will be needed before trying to find out.

● Arrange the children in pairs or threes and give each group just one sheet of A4 paper. Tell them they can use just the paper, a ruler and a calculator to work it out, and leave them for a while to consider the problem. If you think they may mark the table then whiteboard markers may be a good resource to have available.

● Discuss the different approaches to the problem. For example, some children may use the paper as a non-standard ruler. If you have a 'standard' sized table of 1200mm by 600mm then they will probably tell you that it is about eleven and a half sheets. Some may measure both table and paper and then use the calculator to divide one area by another.

Activity development

● Develop the idea of dividing one area by another but insist that the children measure in millimetres. An A4 sheet of paper is 297mm high by 210mm wide. This gives an area of 62 370mm². Many children (and adults) have difficulty with the large numbers which arise when measuring in millimetres. However, this is the main unit for measuring length in science, engineering and the building industry.

● Provide each pair with photocopiable page 109. Explain to them that all measurements are in millimetres. You may like to make the other paper sizes available now, for checking and as a visual aid; alternatively, they can be kept for the review.

Review

● Demonstrate to the children that paper sizes in 'A' size format are unique in that they retain their proportions when cut in half. We may take this for granted, but it is worth demonstrating that it is not true of other sized pieces of paper, such as that used in the USA or for school exercise books. Explain to them that this means there is no waste when cutting.

Learning objectives
(Y5) Use/apply strand: Explore patterns, properties and relationships and propose a general statement involving numbers or shapes.
(Y5) Measure strand: Draw and measure lines to the nearest millimetre; measure and calculate the perimeter of regular and irregular polygons; use the formula for the area of a rectangle to calculate its area.
(Y6) Measure strand: Use standard metric units of measure and convert between units using decimals to two places (eg change 2.75 litres to 2750ml, or vice versa).

Expected prior knowledge
● Understand measurement using mm.
● Work confidently with large numbers.

You will need
A4 paper (one sheet per pair/group of three); rulers (one per pair/group of three); calculators (one per pair/group of three); whiteboard markers (optional); photocopiable page 109 (one per pair); A3, A2 and A1 paper (one sheet per pair or for demonstration only).

Key vocabulary
portrait, landscape (for the orientation of paper)

Brainteaser link
17. Paper folding

Next steps
● Ask the children to calculate the ratio of height to width for each size in their table. They will find they are all the same. The value is approximately 1.41. It is actually the square root of 2.

Paper sizes

A4 paper is the size of this activity sheet. It is 297mm high and 210mm wide.
Measure this page to check.
If you cut A4 in half you get A5 size. If you join two pieces of A4 together you get A3 size. The diagram below shows this arrangement.

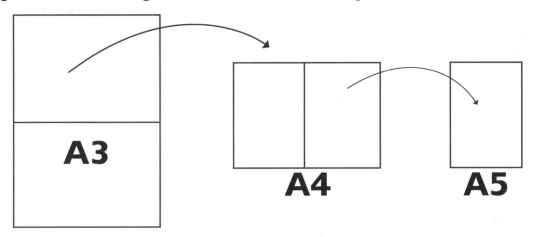

You can carry on cutting paper in half or joining two pieces together, to get other sizes in the sequence.
Complete this table for paper sizes from A0 to A6. The paper is always measured in portrait mode – it is taller than it is wide.

Paper sizes

	A0	A1	A2	A3	A4	A5	A6
Height in mm					297		
Width in mm					210		

◾ How many A4 sheets can you get if you cut up an A0 sheet?

_____

◾ A6 is sometimes called postcard size. How many postcards could you cut from an A0 sheet?

_____

◾ A0 is one square metre in area. Use a calculator to find the area of A0 in your table. How close is it to one square metre?

_____

◾ Find some examples of the larger paper sizes in your classroom. Use your table to work out which paper size it is.

Paper weight

Learning objectives
(Y6) Use/apply strand:
Solve multi-step problems, and problems involving fractions and decimals; choose and use appropriate (and efficient) calculation strategies at each stage, including calculator use.
(Y6) Measure strand:
Select and use standard metric units of measure and convert between units using decimals to two places.

Expected prior knowledge
● Show familiarity with metric units of length, area and mass.
● Measure each of the above accurately.

You will need
Photocopiable page 111 (one per pair); paper for jottings; calculators; information on the area of the classroom (work this out prior to the lesson); a ream of unopened photocopying paper with both 500 sheets and 80gsm written on the end; appropriate scales to weigh the ream of paper (the mass is 2.5kg).

Key vocabulary
ream

Activity introduction
● The main activity is demanding. It requires children to make use of measures in unfamiliar contexts. This introduction makes sure that certain pre-requisite skills are in place.
● Ask: *How much do you weigh, measured in bags of crisps?* Allow them time to unpick the question and decide what information is needed. A typical bag of crisps weighs 25g. The mass of a typical child is around 40kg. Invite the children to discuss the steps needed to find the answer. (1kg is 40 packets, 40 × 40 = 1600 bags of crisps).
● Continue with: How many sheets of paper are needed to cover this classroom? (Calculate the area of the classroom prior to the lesson.) This will entail the children deciding which sheets of paper to use and knowing or measuring the dimensions of the classroom. Make sure the children understand the steps required to reach the answer.

Activity development
● Give each pair a copy of photocopiable page 111, a calculator and some paper for jottings. Emphasise the need to make sure that their answers are sensible at each stage of the activity.
● Explain that the final part of the activity involves weighing a packet of photocopying paper. They must make sure their answer is sensible before they weigh it. Pass the ream around and ask each pair to jot down an estimate of its mass. Explain the markings on the end of the packet.
● Set up space for weighing the ream away from the children, so that it becomes a special part of the lesson.

Review
● Discuss the stages of the activity. Some useful answers are: the 10cm by 10cm square has a mass of 0.8g; a page of A4 has an area of 623.7cm² and weighs 5g. In addition, 16 sheets of paper cover one square metre. (This is a definition of A4 paper – A0 has an area of one square metre and each A size is subsequently halved.)
● When discussing the children's solutions make sure that they are sensible. Some may have had difficulty converting between units. This sometimes leads to calculations that are out by factors of 10, 100 or even 1000.

Next steps
● Pose the following problems: Suppose it is possible to make your ream of paper water tight, by covering it in cling-film. Would it float in water? Ask children to explain their reasoning.
● A litre of water has a mass of 1kg (1000g) and a volume of 1000cm³. The ream would float because its mass is 2500g but its volume is approximately 21 × 30 × 5 cm³, or just over 3000cm³. Its density is therefore about 0.83, less than that of water. This can make a dramatic end to the lesson. Cover the paper in cling-film and place it in water. Many children will not believe that the ream will float until they see it happening.

Paper weight

On the side of a packet of photocopying paper, you might see written '80gsm'.
This means that each square metre of paper has a mass of 80g.

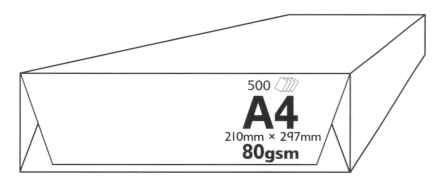

◢ Use this information to work out the mass of a 10cm by 10cm square.

◢ Find the area of one sheet of A4 paper.

◢ How many sheets are needed to cover one square metre?

◢ Calculate the mass of one sheet of A4 paper to the nearest gram.

◢ Use all of the information above to calculate the mass of a ream of paper.

Unusual measuring

Learning objectives
(Y5) Measure strand: Read, choose, use and record standard metric units to estimate and measure length, weight and capacity to a suitable degree of accuracy; convert larger to smaller units using decimals to one place (eg change 2.6kg to 2600g).
(Y5) Measure strand: Draw and measure lines to the nearest millimetre; use the formula for the area of a rectangle to calculate its area.
(Y5) Knowledge strand: Use knowledge of rounding, place value and number facts to estimate and to check calculations.

Expected prior knowledge
● Show confidence with the use of metric units for length, area and mass, including the use of mm².

You will need
A small object with a mass of 50g-200g (such as a stone or a jar); photocopiable page 113 (one per pair); a range of measuring instruments to support their discussions, including stopwatches, balances and scales, metre sticks and rulers; access to information sources, such as the internet (to allow children to check some of their estimates).

Key vocabulary
length - metre, centimetre, millimetre
area - square metre, square centimetre, square millimetre
mass - gram, kilogram
time - hour, minute, second, millisecond; rounding

Activity introduction
● Ask the children how high they think the ceiling of the classroom is in millimetres (mm).
● Discuss the fact that you have used an unusual unit of measurement, which makes it more difficult. Invite them to suggest a strategy for working out the answer.
● Following the discussion, produce a metre stick to help them decide an appropriate figure in metres. If necessary, ask a child to measure. Allow them time to discuss converting this to mm.
● Explain that you are looking for an approximate answer and that the aim is to get close using the rule or metre stick and then to convert to mm. If necessary, they should round their answer appropriately.
● Produce a small object such as a stone or a jar (one with a mass of 50g-200g). Ask them to estimate its mass in kg. Allow them to handle the object and discuss the problems. The aim is to use familiar units and then to convert to unfamiliar ones.

Activity development
● Give out copies of photocopiable page 113 to each pair. Remind them that the units they see are often not the ones most likely to be used to measure an object, and this can lead to very small or very large numbers.
● To illustrate this, ask the children to estimate the area of the table in m² and then in mm². It may come as a surprise that there are one million square millimetres in one square metre. Suggest that they estimate in familiar units first and then convert into unfamiliar ones. Remind them that one item in each list does not have a partner.
● If the children are likely to find the activity too demanding, restrict them to just two or three of the lists. Alternatively, reveal that it is the last item in each list that does not have a partner.

Review
● The focus should first be on asking the children about their estimates for each items. There needs to be some agreement here before the items can be matched.
● The following are the items and measurements which don't have a partner:
  In the first list, the car (approximately 4m or 5m) and 200m, are not used.
  In the second list, the classroom floor is not listed and 300m² is the odd one out.
  The third list can be made easier by converting 20 000 milliseconds into 20 seconds and 0.2 hours into 12 minutes.
  Counting to 1000 and a measurement of 150 seconds are not used.
  Finally, a box of cornflakes (at 1kg) and 3000g are not used.

Next steps
● Ask the children to produce appropriate entries, using unusual units, for the un-partnered items. They might also want to add an entry of their own and choose an unusual unit of measurement for it.

Name _____

Unusual measuring

■ Join each of the items listed to its correct measure with a line. The items are measured in unusual units. In each category, one of the items does not match with a measurement. Decide which item this is and add an appropriate value for it

Length

height of a door	200mm
length of a new pencil	2000cm
height of a tall tree	200m
length of a car	200cm

Area

a football pitch	300m²
a compact disc (CD)	0.062m²
an A4 sheet of paper	5000m²
a classroom floor	11 300mm²

Time

eat a biscuit	150s
walk a kilometre	20 000ms
count to 1000	180min
watch a long film	0.2hr

Mass

a small car	5000kg
a bag of crisps	3000g
a box of cornflakes	1 200 000g
a large elephant	0.03kg

Getting to school

Learning objectives

(Y6) Data strand: Solve problems involving selecting, processing, presenting and interpreting data; draw conclusions and identify further questions to ask.
(Y6) Data strand: Interpret pie charts.
(Y6/Y7) Data strand: Interpret and compare graphs and diagrams that represent data, for example compare proportions in two pie charts that represent different totals.

Expected prior knowledge

● Describe the essential characteristics of a pie chart.
● Use a protractor.

You will need

Photocopiable page 115 (one per child); protractors (one per child); calculators (one per child); OHP or whiteboard.

Key vocabulary

hypothesis, pie chart

Activity introduction

● Remind the children about pie charts and their purpose. They are an efficient way of displaying data but they can be misleading. Each pie chart shows how each of the items in question relate to each other, but it is hard to compare one pie chart with another.
● Tell the children the following story: *Eight girls and six boys were asked what they thought about lunchtime. Of the eight girls, four said lunchtime was too short, three said it was about right and one said it was too long.* Discuss representing this data on a pie chat. Draw a sketch of this chart by dividing a circle into eight equal parts.
● Continue with: *Of the six boys, four said lunchtime was too short, one said it was about right and one said it was too long.* Discuss this data and then represent it on a pie chart with six equal divisions.
● Invite the children to comment on the charts. Ask them to explain why, although there are four girls and four boys who say lunchtime is too short, their respective sectors are different in size.

Activity development

● Provide each child with photocopiable page 115 and a protractor; calculators may also be used if available. Encourage the children to examine the data carefully before answering the questions.
● If they need more support, show them that both the number of Year 6 children and the number of Year 7 children are factors of 360. This means they can work out how much space represents one child in each case.
● The table below shows the data used to construct the pie charts on photocopiable page 115. A key learning objective for this lesson is for the children to understand how to compare two sets of data when the sample sizes are very different.
● Children should also begin to understand how to use the context of the data to answer a question. For example, a possible reason that a larger proportion of Year 7 travel by bus is that secondary age children usually travel further to school than primary age children.

	Year 6	Year 7
Walk	19	72
Bus	8	54
Bicycle	7	48
Taxi	2	6
Totals	36	180

Review

● On an OHP or whiteboard, draw for the whole class a copy of the table at the bottom of photocopiable page 115. Invite the children to suggest an entry for a particular cell. Emphasise the need to explain how they worked out their answer. It is likely that some children will offer solutions that are close but not identical to those shown above.

Next steps

● Investigate a hypothesis, such as: *As children get older, they watch more television.* Identify suitable questions to ask the children and discuss a sensible way to represent the data.

Getting to school

A Year 7 class wanted to test the hypothesis that more secondary school children are likely to walk to school than primary school children. The children questioned 180 Year 7 children and 36 Year 6 children. The results are set out in the pie charts below.

Look at each chart carefully before answering the questions.

Year 6: 36 children

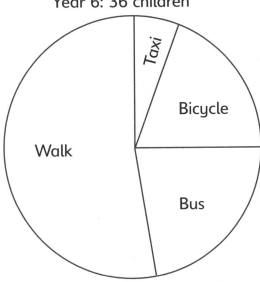

Year 7: 180 children

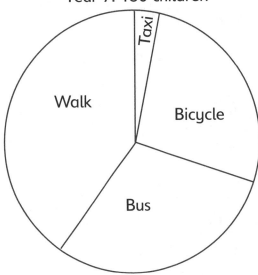

■ Estimate the numbers of Year 6 and Year 7 children who walk to school.

■ Are Year 6 or Year 7 children more likely to walk to school? Use your answers to the two questions above to explain your answer.

■ Give a reason why a larger proportion of Year 7 children than Year 6 children catch the bus.

■ The children collected the data in tables, but the tables are now lost.

■ Try to work out what each entry should be and complete the tables.

■ Discuss with a partner a few ways to improve the accuracy of the survey. Decide if there is a better way to present the findings.

	Year 6	Year 7
Walk		
Bus		
Bicycle		
Taxi		
Totals	36	180

How strong is a bridge?

Learning objectives
(Y5) Data strand: (Determine the data needed to) answer a set of related questions by selecting and organising relevant data; using ICT to present (and highlight) features, and identify further questions to ask.
(Y6) Use/apply strand: Tabulate systematically the information in a problem or puzzle.
(Y6) Data strand: Construct and interpret line graphs.

Expected prior knowledge
● Work independently.
● Collect data from an experiment.

You will need
2cm linking cubes; G clamp (or some means of fastening a cube to the edge of the table); photocopiable page 117 (one per pair); 50g masses; squared paper.

Key vocabulary
mass, scale

Activity introduction
● Fasten a cube to the edge of a table with the connecting lug pointing horizontally away from the table. A clamp is best, but strong sticky tape will do. Connect a second cube to the first by pushing it onto the lug. Continue with a third cube.
● At this point, invite the children to speculate what will happen as you continue to add more cubes, each extending out horizontally from the top of the table.
● Most children will expect the unsupported extension of cubes to break at some point. Allow them to guess how many cubes could be added before they break away. (If you are securing the cube with tape, they may suggest that the tape will give way.)
● Discuss how the experiment could be made fair. For example: *Does it matter how hard you push each cube onto the end of the others?* Attempting to be fair when testing something in this way is important. Rigorous testing is not possible under these conditions, but children should try to avoid creating problems, by following some simple agreed rules.
● Extend the cubes until they fall away. Allow some time for the children to discuss and agree what happened.

Activity development
● Explain that today they are going to make a bridge.
● Give each pair approximately 30 linking cubes and a copy of photocopiable page 117. If necessary, show them how to make the towers that will be used for all of the bridges. These are four bricks arranged so that the top of each tower can hold the span in place.
● Discuss possible sizes of spans for the bridge. Explain that the span is the total length of the bridge, not the gap between the towers. The activity involves placing 50g masses on the span to see if it bends or breaks. A span of four cubes is needed before the bricks can break under strain. However, if the 50g masses are rather large this size of span may be too small to give a meaningful result. Hence the bridge experiment starts with a span of five cubes. This means that there will be three bricks between the towers and one on top of each tower.
● Give out squared paper for the final part of the activity.

Review
● A key point of interest in this review is for the children to discuss not only their results but also the reliability and integrity of their data. The results should show that bridges become weaker as they get larger.

Next steps
● The children should discuss the reliability of their data. Can the strength of the bridge be affected by how hard you push the cubes together, or if you place the masses on the centre very gently? As the span size increases, is there a point where the bridge will hold no additional mass at all and collapses under its own weight? Is there a case for taking several measurements of each experiment and using the average?

How strong is a bridge?

■ Make a simple bridge from linking cubes. Here are the building instructions.

The bridge is made with two support towers, each four cubes high.
The bridge has a simple span, made by joining ten cubes together.

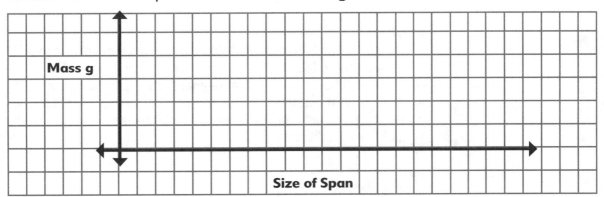

■ Place a 50g mass in the centre of your bridge and see if it bends or breaks.

■ If it is secure, then place another 50g mass. Continue this process until the span gives way. If necessary, use smaller masses to get a better result.

Experiment with spans of different sizes and record your results in the table below. You may want to rebuild each span and repeat the experiment to check the result.

Span size

	5	6	7	8	9	10	11	12	13	14	15	16	17	18	19	20
Mass g																

■ Using squared paper, draw a graph (like the one below) which shows your results. You need to put the scale for mass in yourself.

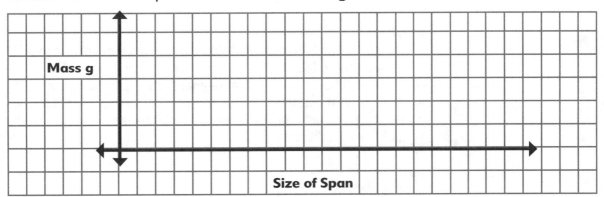

Mass g

Size of Span

■ Comment on the shape of your graph. What can you tell about the strength of the span? Write your comments here.

_____

_____

Toppling cubes

Activity introduction

- Some children may find a written explanation of the activity on photocopiable page 119 a little difficult. Therefore this introduction is concerned with explaining the experimental side of the activity.
- Invite the children to take three bricks and to connect them to make an L shape, ensuring that none of the small lugs used to join the cubes are at the ends of the L. Place the L shape on the table upside down. It should balance and not topple over.
- Invite the children to speculate how the L could be made larger. It must be able to rest upside down without toppling. For example, they could increase the height, increase the width or increase both of them.
- Ask each pair of children to make a variety of L shapes and to find one that will rest on its end, upside down. Ask them to note the height of the L and the width of the L.

Activity development

- Ask the children how they could record the results of the introductory activity. They need to see easily which of the L shapes topple and which do not. If the children do not suggest it, move them towards notation for the L shape, based on height and width, and a simple *yes* or *no* in answer to the question, *Does it topple?*
- Hand out copies of photocopiable page 119. Explain that the children can use the table as a method of recording their results.
- There may be examples where the L shape topples some times and not others. These cases will need to be treated very carefully. Remind the children to make sure that they do not try to balance the L shape on the small lug used to join cubes together.
- Before the children begin the activity, take the opportunity to discuss 'fair testing'. In order for the result to be reliable, children will need to be careful with the way they join cubes together, and to rest each one in the same way on a reliably flat surface.

Review

- Gather the children together to discuss results. The focus should be on allowing them to describe the observations they made after collecting results. If there is disagreement, then have some cubes available so that everyone can agree a particular result. There are no answers offered here for this activity as a lot depends on the specific type of linking cube used.

Next steps
- Explore what happens with L shapes that are twice as thick as the normal cubes. You will need to make large cubes from eight small ones for this experiment.

Learning objectives
(Y5) Data strand: Answer a set of related questions by collecting, selecting and organising relevant data; using ICT to present (and highlight) features and identify further questions to ask.
(Y6) Use/apply strand: Tabulate systematically the information in a problem or puzzle.

Expected prior knowledge
- Understand how to carry out an experiment, largely independently.

You will need
Photocopiable page 119; 2cm linking cubes (approx. 50 per pair).

Key vocabulary
stability, balance (some children may understand the term 'centre of mass' or the less precise term, 'centre of gravity')

Toppling cubes

◖ With a partner, use linking cubes to make a variety of different **L** shapes. Place each one upside down and see if it will balance.

◖ Record your results in the table below. If an **L** shape balances upside down, then place a tick in the cell. If it does not, then place a cross there.

		Width of L Shape										
		2	**3**	**4**	**5**	**6**	**7**	**8**	**9**	**10**	**11**	**12**
Height of L Shape	**2**											
	3											
	4											
	5											
	6											
	7											
	8											
	9											
	10											
	11											
	12											

◖ Use your table to write a short explanation of your results.

How fast is that?

Activity introduction
● Tell the children that sometimes your car travels at 1km per minute. Ask them how many km per hour that is. Give them time to think and discuss their answers. Now ask them to explain what a speed of 60km per hour would mean if you were to travel at that speed. This question may sound straightforward, but many children find the concept of speed difficult to grasp.
● Return to the speed of 1km per minute and ask them what speed this is in metres per second. Suggest that they round their answer appropriately. After you have gained the correct answer (16.67m/s, 16.7m/s or 17m/s, depending on how they choose to round the answer), explain that this means that this distance is covered every second. Ask them if they think this speed is reached by a sprinter, a racehorse or a cheetah. In fact an Olympic male 100m sprinter can reach about 11m/s, a racehorse can reach 16-18m/s and a cheetah can reach about 30m/s.

Activity development
● Return to the question about your car travelling 1km in one minute and make sure that all children can perform the necessary calculation to give a speed in m/s.
● Write the following on the board:
A speed boat travels 2.4km in one minute and 23.5 seconds. What is the speed in m/s?
● Give the children some time to discuss the units the problem is posed in, the notation used, and then to decide what calculations are needed to solve the problem.
● Invite them to convert the distance into 2400m and the time into 83.5s. The speed of the boat will be 2400/83.5=28.7m/s. Hand out copies of photocopiable page 121 and ensure that they understand the aim of the activity (to calculate running speeds for men's world records over a range of distances).

Review
● Discuss the answers to the calculations. Establish that the speeds go down gradually from the top of the table to the bottom. Ask them why this is. Invite the children to speculate what would happen if the distance became much longer.

Learning objectives
(Y6) Use/apply strand: Solve multi-step problems, and problems involving fractions, decimals and percentages; choose and use appropriate calculation strategies at each stage, including calculator use.
(Y6) Measure strand: Compare readings on different scales
(Y6) Data strand: Describe and interpret results and solutions to problems using the mode, range, median and mean.

Expected prior knowledge
● Convert minutes and seconds into seconds.
● Understand that speed is found by taking the total distance travelled and dividing by the time taken.

You will need
Calculators (one per child); photocopiable page 121.

Key vocabulary
distance, speed, velocity, average

Next steps
● Invite the children to use the internet to make a similar table for the women's world records.
● Alternatively, ask them to make a chart of animal speeds. An interesting display could be created in which a length of string is stretched to represent the distance travelled by an animal in one second.

How fast is that?

◧ Here are the men's world record times for running:
The races range from 100m to 10000m.
The average speed of a runner is found by dividing the total distance by the total time for the race.

1. Complete the table. The 800 metres data has been filled in for you.

Distance (metres)	Time	Time in seconds	Average speed (m/s)
100	9.77s		
200	19.32s		
400	43.18s		
800	1:41.11	101.11	7.9
1000	2:11.96		
1500	3:26.00		
3000	7:20.67		
5000	12:37.53		
10000	26:17.53		

2. Write a short passage commenting on how the average speed of these records changes depending on the length of the race.

Dicing with probability (1)

Activity introduction

- Show the children a normal die. (Most people use the term *dice* to represent both the singular (die) and the plural.) Ask them for the probability of scoring a 6 when the dice is thrown. Ask: *Is this the same as the probability of scoring a 3* (or any other number)?
- Continue by asking them the probability of scoring; a) 7, b) an even number, c) a number less than 7. These questions are designed to make sure the children understand the extent of the 0-1 probability number line.
- On a blank dice, write the numbers 0, 2, 3, 3, 4, 4 with a red marker pen. Ask: *What is the probability that a throw with this dice produce an even number?* (You may need to explain that zero is an even number.) Continue by asking for the probability of throwing an odd number. Ask them what they notice about the sum of these two answers. Encourage them to explain why the total of these two probabilities is 1.

Activity development

- If the children are confident with the concept of probability, then give out photocopiable page 123 to each pair.
- Alternatively, introduce activity on the photocopiable page as a whole class activity by keeping the first dice (marked in red) from the introduction and on another blank dice write the numbers 1, 1, 2, 2, 8, 8 with a blue marker pen.
- Allow them to play the game several times to help them decide which dice is the 'better'. On photocopiable page 123, there is a recording grid. Adjacent to the grid, there is space for the children to convert their results into probabilities. Some children will need additional support to realise that the recording grid has all possibilities, and therefore they can find the probability for each dice by simply counting how often it appears in the grid, and then dividing by 36.

Review

- Invite the children to share their probabilities for each dice. The results are shown in the table. Red = 18/36, Blue 16/36 and Draw 2/36. The two dice are quite evenly matched and the children may not notice much of a difference simply by playing the game. Explain to them that they may need to play many times

		Blue dice					
		1	1	2	2	8	8
Red dice	0	B	B	B	B	B	B
	2	R	R	X	X	B	B
	3	R	R	R	R	B	B
	3	R	R	R	R	B	B
	4	R	R	R	R	B	B
	4	R	R	R	R	B	B

before it becomes apparent that the red dice is better, despite the fact that it has a zero and no numbers to match the 8 on the blue dice.

Next steps

- Invite the children to alter the numbers on the two dice so that they are fair. Tell them that they must have different numbers on each of the two dice. Although this is a demanding task, it is one which the children can access using a grid like the one above.

Learning objectives

(Y5) Data strand: Describe the occurrence of familiar events using the language of chance or likelihood.
(Y6) Data strand: Describe and predict outcomes from data using the language of chance or likelihood.
(Y6/Y7) Data strand: Understand and use the probability scale from 0 to 1; find and justify probabilities based on equally likely outcomes in simple contexts.

Expected prior knowledge

- Understand the 0-1 probability number line in which 0 represents an impossible event and 1 represents a certain event.

You will need

Photocopiable page 123 (one per pair); two blank dice (one per pair), a red marker pen and a blue marker pen, suitable for marking the dice (if blank dice are not available, then use hexagonal spinners).

Key vocabulary

probability, outcome

Brainteaser link:

15. Dice with a difference

Dicing with probability (1)

◾ Two blank dice, or spinners, are needed for this game.

◾ On one dice, write the numbers 0, 2, 3, 3, 4, 4 in red.

◾ On the other dice, write the numbers 1, 1, 2, 2, 8, 8 in blue.

◾ One player throws the red dice and the other throws the blue dice. The winner is the player with the highest score. If it is a draw, then throw again.

◾ Decide which is the best dice to use, and explain your reasoning below. Play the game several times before you decide.

◾ To help you, complete this table displaying all of the possibilities for the two dice. Look at the two possible scores and put in an R if the red dice wins, B if the blue dice wins and X if it is a draw.

		Blue dice					
		1	1	2	2	8	8
Red dice	0						
	2						
	3						
	3						
	4						
	4						

Total wins for red: _____

Total wins for blue: _____

Draws: _____

Probabilities

Red win = $\dfrac{}{36}$

Blue win = $\dfrac{}{36}$

Draw = $\dfrac{}{36}$

The best dice to use is _____

because _____

_____

_____

Dicing with probability (2)

Activity introduction

● Show the children an ordinary die (dice). Ask them to add the numbers on its six faces. Once they give you the total of 21, explain that they have a blank dice and can write any numbers on it. However, the total of these must also be 21. The aim is to produce a dice to beat the standard 1-6 dice. Explain that you will play a game over 18 throws (or 36 if there is time) and that you will keep a record of which dice wins each time. Give them time to think of suitable numbers and to experiment with their total of 21.

● Once they are ready, tell them that you will roll your dice and then every child will roll theirs. They can record a win, lose, or draw. The difficulty here is deciding if a win by a child is good luck, or based on good mathematics. They may want to investigate further by extending the experiment. Alternatively, draw up a grid like the one below.

Learning objectives
(Y5) Data strand: Describe the occurrence of familiar events using the language of chance or likelihood.
(Y6) Data strand: Describe and predict outcomes from data using the language of chance or likelihood.
(Y6/Y7) Data strand: Understand and use the probability scale from 0 to 1; find and justify probabilities based on equally likely outcomes in simple contexts.

Expected prior knowledge
● Understand the 0-1 probability number line where 0 represents an impossible event and 1 represents a certain event. (It would be helpful if the children had already worked on Lesson 48 'Dicing with probability (1).)

You will need
Ordinary dice; three blank dice (per group of three) and one extra (per child) for the introduction; red, blue, and green marker pens, suitable for marking the dice (if blank dice are not available then use hexagonal spinners, preferably on card coloured red, blue and green); photocopiable page 125 (one per child).

Key vocabulary
probability, outcome

Activity development

● Show the children the numbers for the three dice on photocopiable page 125. Explain that they are going to carry out an experiment with these dice to see which will produce the most highest numbers in the game.

● Encourage the children to work systematically with pairs of dice at a time, and to record their observations after 36 throws.

		Dice B					
		3	3	5	5	7	7
Dice A	1	B	B	B	B	B	B
	1	B	B	B	B	B	B
	6	A	A	A	A	B	B
	6	A	A	A	A	B	B
	8	A	A	A	A	A	A
	8	A	A	A	A	A	A

● If the children have confidence with this, suggest that they can make their comparisons by using a recording grid. The grid for Dice A against Dice B is shown on the right. The letter of the winning dice is recorded. In the case on the right, Dice A beats Dice B with 20 wins out of 36 to 16 wins out of 36.

Review

● Invite the children to share their experimental results. To make a convincing argument, show them tables like the one above for all pairs of dice. Some children may discover early on that these dice do not behave as they would expect. The surprising result holds that Dice A beats Dice B, Dice B beats Dice C, and Dice C beats Dice A. The dice can be used in a contest by allowing your opponent to choose first. You can then choose the dice that beats it! This result, known as non-transitive, is counter intuitive and offers lots of avenues for the curious to explore.

Next steps
● Invite the children to investigate four dice with the following arrangement of numbers.
A) 0, 0, 4, 4, 4, 4
B) 3, 3, 3, 3, 3, 3
C) 2, 2, 2, 2, 6, 6
D) 1, 1, 1, 5, 5, 5
These amazing dice have the same non-transitive property as those above. A beats B, B beats C, C beats D and D beats A.

Name _____

Dicing with probability (2)

◀ Mark three blank dice using these numbers. Use hexagonal spinners if dice are not available.

Dice A: 1, 1, 6, 6, 8, 8
Dice B: 3, 3, 5, 5, 7, 7
Dice C: 2, 2, 4, 4, 9, 9

◀ Play a simple dice game in which three players each take one of the dice.

◀ Play against each other, two at a time. Each player rolls their dice 36 times and records who wins (rolls the highest number) on each throw. The winner is the dice with the most highest throws.

The aim is to try this with different combinations of pairs of dice and to decide which dice is the best.

◀ Record your results after 36 throws.

Game 1 Dice A _____ Dice B _____

Game 2 Dice B _____ Dice C _____

Game 3 Dice C _____ Dice A _____

◀ Describe your results here. Which of the three dice A, B or C is the best one?

◀ Comment on anything strange about your results.

Probable pairs

Activity introduction

- Say: *Some people think that the number 6 is the hardest number to throw with a die (or dice). Is this true?* Give them time to discuss the statement and invite comments. They may observe that a 6 is often wanted to start or finish a game, and the extra focus on this makes it seem harder to throw.
- Ask the children to test the statement by giving them a dice each and asking them to throw it 20 times and make a tally chart. Ask: *Are there any patterns in your results?* Combine all of the marks from the group into one large chart. Ask again if they notice any patterns. Given that the number six should appear approximately 1/6 of the time, each bar in your chart should be about the same length.
- Conclude by explaining that each of the numbers on a dice is as likely to come up as any other; they are all equally likely events.

Activity development

- Tell the children that a survey was carried out on 60 families with two children. Using careful wording, ask them to estimate how many families would have two boys, how many two girls and how many one of each.
- Many children will assume that two boys, two girls and one of each are all equally likely events, and suggest that about 20 families will be in each group. Give each pair a copy of photocopiable page 127 and a coin, and explain how it is to be used. If time is short, then give each pair two coins and show them how they can throw both and tally the results quickly.
- If any children recognise at once that there will be twice as many families with one of each as there will be with two boys or two girls, you could move them straight on to 'Next steps'.

Review

- Ask the children to comment on their results. Many children should have results that contradict their original assumptions about equally likely events. Invite them to explain why there are about twice as many families with 'one of each' than with either two boys or two girls.
- Put all of the results together to make a large graph. It should show the 1:2:1 proportions more accurately.
- Conclude by asking the children the same question asked at the start of the 'Activity development'.

Learning objectives
(Y6) Data strand: Describe and predict outcomes from data using the language of chance or likelihood.
(Y6) Data strand: Solve problems by selecting, processing, presenting and interpreting data; draw conclusions and identify further questions to ask.
(Y6/Y7) Data strand: Understand and use the probability scale from 0 to 1; find and justify probabilities based on equally likely outcomes in simple contexts.

Expected prior knowledge
- Understand simple probability.
- Understand tally charts and their use as a tool for collecting data.

You will need
Photocopiable page 127; some dice and coins for each pair of children.

Key vocabulary
tally chart, probability, equally likely outcomes

Brainteaser link
15. Dice with a difference

Next steps
- Investigate the likely distribution of children in families with three or four children. They could extend the diagram used on photocopiable page 127 to help, or invent a recording method of their own. With three children, three girls and three boys each have a probability of 1/8. Two boys and a girl, and two girls and a boy, each have a probability of 3/8. For four children, four of a kind has a probability of 1/16, three of a kind and one other has a probability of 4/16 or 1/4, and two of each has a probability of 6/16 or 3/8.

Name _____

Probable pairs

1. Start at the top of the path and toss a coin. If the coin falls 'head up', move down the path for a girl. If it falls 'tail up', move down the path for a boy.

2. Toss the coin again and, in the same way, move down the lower paths.

3. Mark a tally for two girls, one boy and one girl, or two boys.

4. After 60 goes, draw a graph of the results and write a short comment underneath.

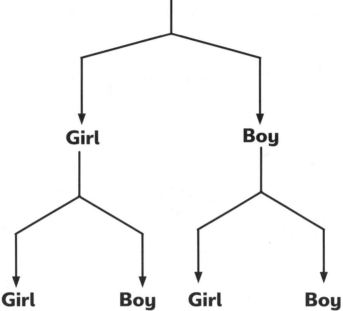

Tally			
	Two Girls	One Boy One Girl	Two Boys

Graph

Number

               Two Girls   One Boy One Girl   Two Boys